I. INTRODUCTION

The United States' relationship with the People's Republic of China (PRC) has evolved over the past thirty-five years from one of armed conflict, through a cautious period of detente, and into the present era of limited but developing cooperation. China's armed forces, the largest in the world, remain of great interest and importance.[1] While studies of China's legal system have appeared in the West with increasing frequency, surprisingly little has been written concerning its military legal system.[2] Admittedly, several difficulties arise in attempting such a study. Until recently, the primary problem with studying Chinese law has been one of finding it. Especially during the Cultural Revolution (1966-1976), law was virtually entirely displaced by rule through policies and directives of the Chinese Communist Party (CCP). Secondly, sensitivity about "state secrets" is especially acute in the PRC. Documents concerning the military, to include military law, are generally classified, and relatively few have emerged from China. Nevertheless, from those source documents which have become available, from official policy statements, and from accounts of military trials, an adequate representation may be drawn of the development, structure and function of the military legal system of Communist China.[3]

The general functions of a system of military law are to govern the persons within the military and to maintain discipline so as to assure the accomplishment of assigned tasks.[4] The functions of the Chinese Communist military legal structure are significantly broader, largely due to the unqiue political characteristics of the Chinese People's Liberation Army (PLA). As Mao Tse-tung[5] wrote in 1929, "the Chinese Red Army is an armed body for carrying out the political tasks of the revolution."[6] The role of military law and discipline thus assumes a broader aspect in this politicized army, which is reflected in the definition of military discipline from the authoritative Chinese military dictionary Ci Hai:

1

A standard with which the armed forces must comply to guarantee political, organizational, and operational consistency. The military discipline of the Chinese People's Liberation Army is based on political consciousness and is the guarantee that the revolutionary line will be carried out. It is a basic factor in combat effectiveness.[7]

As will be shown herein, there are two main functions of the Chinese Communist military legal system: (1) to maintain a high degree of political unity between the CCP and the PLA; and (2) to maintain military order and discipline and thereby increase military potential. In response to changed political conditions or periods of crisis, the military legal system has on occasion been called upon to enlarge its legal and administrative jurisdictions to include the civil sector under its authority. Military Tribunals of Military Control Committees have constituted the legal authority for large areas of Communist China during significant periods of its history, when conditions of what may be termed "martial law" prevailed. At the same time, the military legal system has had the continuing task of maintaining order and discipline within the PLA itself.

This thesis will examine the development, structure and function of the Chinese Communist military legal system in its broader sense, to include its political and martial law roles. To limit this study to an artificially narrow examination of the maintenance of internal discipline alone would distort the significance and role of military law in Communist China.

II. HISTORICAL FRAMEWORK

In order to understand the role of the military legal system of Communist China, it is first necessary to gain a basic appreciation of certain concepts within the broader millieu of traditional Chinese law. The

2

legal system of the People's Republic of China is not merely communist law, but also Chinese law. Although the legal system of the PRC has drawn heavily from Soviet sources, it also retains, to a significant degree, many of the distinctive features of China's own legal heritage. It must, therefore, be analyzed in the context of Chinese history.

Much of China's historical legal development is typified by the continuing tension inherent in a dichotomy of two competing models of law. These models have been labeled, on the one hand, "external,"[8] "formal,"[9] "bureaucratic,"[10] or "jural"[11]; on the other, "internal," "informal," "mobilizational" or "societal." The jural model stands for formalized, codified rules of universal application, enforced by a regularized judicial system. The societal model stands for the application of internalized societal norms and customary values, enforced in a particularized fashion (depending on one's class or social status) by extrajudicial agencies and social organizations.

A.   Traditional Chinese Legal Concepts[12]

The Confucian philosophy which guided traditional China held that upright and benevolent personal behavior and proper observance of social relationships produced societal order and well-being. Upright behavior on the part of individuals would bring ordered harmony in their families, which would in turn lead to well-governed states and, ultimately, world peace.[13] This behavior was governed by li (moral code, or customary law). The preference for moral persuasion and example over rule by harsh punishments and formalized codes was expressed by Confucius:

> Lead the people by laws and regulate them by penalties, and the people will try to keep out of jail, but will have no sense of shame. Lead the people by virtue and restrain them by the rules of decorum (li), and the people will have a sense of shame, and moreover will become good.[14]

The Confucian philosophy was rivalled by the Legalist school of thought, which favored a harsh, punitive system of positive law (fa)[15] in order to maintain public order and create a strong state. The legalists criticized li as being an unstable basis for government "since the li are unwritten, particularistic, and subject to arbitrary interpretation."[16]

While the Confucian philosophy eventually triumphed as the basis of traditional Chinese society, aspects of legalism were incorporated as well. Laws were primarily penal in emphasis, to punish violations of the codified dominant Confucian ethical norms. The law was nevertheless rarely invoked to uphold these norms; only where moral persuasion and societal pressures had failed was the law needed. Law was mainly concerned with those acts of moral impropriety or criminal violence which were seen as violations of the whole social order and, ultimately, the entire harmonious order of the universe. "The belief that disastrous natural phenomena - floods, droughts, tempests, insect pests - were the consequences of human disorder provided further theoretical justification for punishment of wrongdoers: they were a double menace to society."[17]

Because the Chinese legal system was intended to protect societal harmony and punish those who violated the rules of good order and conduct, many of the protections which evolved in western societies to guard the rights of individuals against the state did not develop in China. First, the concept of the presumption that an accused is innocent until proven guilty did not develop in China.[18] Second, there was no principle of equality before the law; rather, differing treatment was accorded based on the relative class and social status of the offender and victim.[19] Third, voluntary surrender and confession, in keeping with Confucian ethics, were strongly encouraged and could be a mitigating factor in criminal cases; on the other hand failure to confess was generally seen as obduracy and could

4

constitute an aggravating factor.[20]   Torture as a means of obtaining a confession during trials was specifically allowed under the penal code of the Ch'ing dynasty (1644-1912).[21]   Fourth, if the laws did not specifically address a given offense or penalty, a magistrate could apply another statute by analogy.[22]   Finally, there were no defense attorneys to assist the accused.   Since the laws penalized as disruptors of tranquility both those who incited others to institute court actions, as well as those who profited from them, the development of a legal profession was problematic.[23]

Due to the harsh, punitive nature of the formal legal system, the people regarded it with distaste and fear. "Don't eat anything poisonous, and don't break the law," ran a Chinese proverb. Or again: "[A]void litigation; for once go to law and there is nothing but trouble."[24] The formal legal system was therefore avoided to the greatest extent possible. To resolve disputes and adjudicate minor offense, an informal legal system of extrajudicial organs and procedures developed, in keeping with the Confucian mandate that tranquility be maximized. The clan (tsu), the guild, councils of local gentry or elders, and other local institutions resolved most conflicts through mediation, conciliation and imposition of minor disciplinary sanctions.[25] These informal, or societal, institutions became the predominant system of dispute resolution in traditional China.

B.   Military Law in Imperial China

Traditional Chinese society displayed a curiously ambivalent attitude toward the profession of arms. While the classical literature is replete with the exploits of ancient warrior heroes, Confucian society had little esteem for the soldier, ranking him fifth in the traditional social hierarchy (after the scholar, the farmer, the artisan and the merchant).[26] "Good iron is not wrought into nails, good men do not become soldiers" ran a Chinese

5

proverb.[27] Nevertheless, seven "martial classics," with Sun Tzu's Art of War pre-eminent among them, are studied to this day.[28]

The antecedents of Chinese military law extend into the deep reaches of antiquity. An Assistant Judge Advocate General of the Republic of China Armed Forces has written that a system of military discipline to facilitate the execution of orders was in existence during China's mythic golden age over four thousand six hundred years ago, "when Hwang-ti waged war with Chi-yu at the battle of Cho Lo, and issued his first regulations."[29] At least a rudimentary system of military law must have been developed by the fourth century B.C., when Sun Tzu's classic The Art of War was compiled. Sun Tzu wrote of the importance to discipline of "consistent rules to guide the officers and men," together with an enlightened system of rewards and punishments to enhance military discipline and loyalty.[30] A traditional system of military regulations developed from these antecedents and served as the basis of the military legal system down through the successive dynastic periods until the establishment of the Republic of China in 1912.

The imperial legal codes contained separate sections devoted to regulating the military. The fifth division of the Ta Ch'ing Lu-li[31] was devoted to "Military Laws," which punished such offenses as divulging state military secrets,[32] unauthorized sale of military material,[33] and desertion.[34] To encourage officers to properly discipline their troops, eighty blows of the bamboo could be adjudged for failing to preserve military law and discipline.[35] On the other hand, the officer who ruled with too heavy a hand could be punished for "exciting and causing rebellion by oppressive conduct," a capital offense.[36]

There was little differentiation between civilian and military in the imperial legal system.   No specialized military courts or tribunals

6

existed.[37] Military defendants, like their civilian counterparts, were tried before the regular court system under the supervision of the imperial government's Board of Punishments.[38] Moreover, punishment under the "Military Laws" of the Ch'ing code was not limited to members of the military. Some of the military laws for which civilians could be punished were: crossing a border without examination at a government border post;[39] divulging state secrets;[40] purchasing military materiel sold without authorization;[41] and harboring deserters.[42] Finally, military personnel were also subject to punishment under laws other than simply those listed under the "Military Laws."[43]

C. Military Law in Republican China (1911 to 1949)

The Hsin-hai revolution of 10 October 1911 led to the overthrow of the Ch'ing dynasty and the establishment of the Republic of China (ROC) in 1912. Dr. Sun Yat-sen, father of the Republic, was committed to the strengthening and modernization of all social institutions, to include China's legal system.[44] The Nationalist government undertook an ambitious program of codifying civil, criminal and commercial laws, based on the codes of France, Germany, Switzerland, and Japan.[45] Many departures from the traditional Chinese system were incorporated into the new codes.[46] Crime by analogy, as well as the Ch'ing code's catch-all section on "doing what ought not to be done" were abolished. In their place was adopted the principle of nullen crimen sine lege (no crime without a preexisting law making the act a crime). The traditional preferential treatment for officials and intellectuals, as well as the use of torture to gain confessions, were prohibited. The development of a modern legal profession was now encouraged. Still, a number of traditional features remained in the new legal system. Significant among them was the continued encouragement of voluntary surrender and confession as potentially mitigating factors.[47]

The extensive codification of civilian law undertaken during the Republican period was paralleled by the development of a military legal system. Regulations promulgated by presidential mandate on 26 March 1915 established a separate system of military courts.[48] While the Regulations established considerable differentiation between the military and the civilian legal system, the jurisdiction of the military courts was fairly broad. Soldiers could be tried by court-martial for violations of the civilian Criminal Code "or any other law providing punishment for its violation."[49] Crimes committed before a soldier joined the service could nevertheless be tried by court-martial, but if crimes committed while in the service were not detected until after the soldier had left the army, the ordinary courts had jurisdiction in most cases.[50]

Military legal developments were rapid following the establishment of the Kuomintang[51] government in 1927. A military criminal law was promulgated in 1929,[52] followed by a military trial procedure law in 1930.[53] The 1934 code of martial law provided for the extension of general military jurisdiction over specified offenses, which could then be tried before military courts or assigned to civilian courts.[54] The Nationalists' military legal development was completed on Taiwan with the adoption in 1956 of a modernized procedural Military Trial Law.[55]

III. FOUNDATIONS OF MILITARY LAW IN COMMUNIST CHINA

A. Marxist-Leninist Concepts of Law

Communist legal theory emphasizes the class nature of law and its subordination to political and economic dictates. Rejecting a stabilizing role for law, Marx and Engels viewed it as a political tool of class rule, created to promote the interests of the ruling classes: "[Y]our

8

jurisprudence is but the will of your class made into a law for all, a will, whose essential character and direction are determined by the economical conditions of existence of your class."[56] Lenin also adopted this view of law: "A law is a political instrument; it is politics."[57]

Under Marxist theory, capitalist society must undergo a "revolutionary transformation" into a communist society, where the state and its laws will wither away. This "political transition period" Marx called "the revolutionary dictatorship of the proletariat."[58] As to the means required to bring about this transformation, Marx declared that there was "only one means to curtail, simplify and localize the bloody agony of the old society and the bloody birth-pangs of the new, only one means—the revolutionary terror."[59] Lenin characterized the dictatorship of the proletarial as "a special kind of cudgel, nothing else,"[60] with which to beat down and crush the exploiting classes. As early as 1901 Lenin fully concurred with Marx's tactics for revolution: "In principle we have never renounced terror and cannot renounce it."[61] Once in power, Lenin actually incorporated terror as a principle of Soviet law. In forwarding his own draft of a proposed article to the 1922 Soviet criminal code, Lenin wrote:

> The main idea . . . [is] to put forward publicly a thesis that is correct in principle and politically (not only strictly juridical), which explains the substance of terror, its necessity and limits, and provides justification for it.
>
> The courts must not ban terror—to promise that would be deception or self-deception—but must formulate the motives underlying it, legalize it as a principle, plainly, without any make-believe or embellishment. It must be formulated in the ¯broadest possible manner, for only revolutionary law and revolutionary conscience can more or less widely determine the limits within which it should be applied.[62]

B.   Chinese Communist Attitudes Toward Law

Mao Tse-tung and the Chinese Communist Party retained, whether consciously or not, many traditional Chinese attitudes toward law. Some of the parallels between traditional and communist Chinese law which will later be addressed with respect to the military legal system include: (1) a preference for informal dispute settlement and punishment for minor offenses; (2) the subordination of law to a dominant political philosophy; and (3) lack of functional separation between law and bureaucracy. Nevertheless, it is from Marxist-Leninist ideology and the Soviet model that the basic concepts and formulations of the Chinese communist legal system were drawn.

In 1927 Mao wrote of the need for excesses, even terror, to break the hold of tradition by revolutionary action:

[A] revolution is not a dinner party, or writing an essay, or painting a picture, or doing embroidery; it cannot be so refined, so leisurely and gentle, so temperate, kind, courteous, restrained and magnanimous. A revolution is an insurrection, an act of violence by which one class overthrows another.... To put it bluntly, it is necessary to create terror for a while in every rural area, or otherwise it would be impossible to suppress the activities of the counter-revolutionaries in the countryside or overthrow the authority of the gentry. Proper limits have to be exceeded in order to right a wrong, or else the wrong cannot be righted.[63]

Once in power, Mao's views of revolutionary legality and class justice remained little changed:

The state apparatus, including the army, the police and the courts, is the instrument by which one class oppresses another. It is an instrument for the oppression of antagonistic classes; it is violence and not "benevolence."[64]

10

The laws adopted in the early periods of the People's Republic of China reflected Mao's class-oriented doctrines. Law was chiefly a weapon to be used in suppressing "counterrevolution" and major crimes:

> The criminal law of our country mainly attacks counterrevolutionary criminals and criminals who murder, commit arson, steal, swindle, rape, and commit other crimes that seriously undermine social order and socialist construction. We must make it clear that the sharp point of our criminal law is mainly directed at the enemies of socialism.[65]

Mao explained his theoretical framework for analyzing and resolving societal conflicts in his 1957 speech "On the Correct Handling of Contradictions Among the People."[66] Mao sharply distinguished "contradictions between ourselves and the enemy" ("antagonisic contradictions") from "contradictions among the people" ("nonantagonistic" contradictions).[67] Mao defined "the people" as those who "favor, support and work for the cause of socialist construction"; "the enemy" were those who "resist the socialist revolution and are hostile to or sabotage socialist construction."[68] Mao also explained the methods to be used in resolving the two types of contradictions. To suppress contradictions involving the enemy, or criminals who "seriously disrupt public order," the methods of "dictatorship" would be applied. To resolve contradictions among the people, "democracy" ("the methods of persuasion and education" and "administrative regulations") would be applied. "Law-breaking elements among the people will be punished according to law, but this is different in principle from the exercise of dictatorship to suppress the enemies of the people."[69] Here the traditional preference for informal or administrative resolution of social conflicts was applied to "contradictions among the people"; minor crimes among the people would be resolved "according to law"; while the full weight of the state was reserved for the suppression of the counterrevolutionary "enemy" and major criminals.

C.   Military Law in the Chinese Workers' and Peasants' Red Army
(1927-1931)

The development of the Chinese Communist system of military law reflects the unique characteristics of the Chinese Communist armed forces. Besides the standard function of maintaining military discipline in order to increase military potential, Chinese Communist military law developed an even greater emphasis on the maintenance of the close political relationship between the military and the Chinese Communist party.

The foundations of the Chinese Communist military legal system were laid early in the history of the CCP, and by the time the People's Republic of China was established in 1949, military law had already undergone considerable development. Commencing as a rather arbitrary and informal process, encompassing civilians as well as the military, the system evolved into one that at least formally differentiated the military from civilian society. Some internal procedural guarantees such as rights of appeal and of review also emerged.   In light of the nearly constant state of revolutionary warfare that prevailed during this period, these developments are remarkable.

The CCP did not immediately organize its own army following its establishment in 1921; rather, it infiltrated and worked within the Kuomintang (KMT) on its "special task to do propagandistic and organizational work among the workers and peasants"[70] behind the lines. With the failure of its "mass line" policy to raise the workers and peasants in revolution following the CCP's Nanchang and Autumn Harvest armed uprisings of 1927, the Party began to develop a new strategy calling for its own army.

12

The CCP had no illusions regarding the necessity of armed struggle to achieve power and accomplish revolution. Mao later wrote: "The seizure of power by armed force, the settlement of the issue by war, is the central task and the highest form of war."[71] The Chinese Communist doctrine of war descended from Clausewitz, through Marx, Engels and Lenin, to Mao. Lenin stated that Clausewitz' famous dictum ("War is merely the continuation of policy by other means"[72]) "was always the standpoint of Marx and Engels, who regarded any war as the continuation of the politics of the powers concerned—and the various classes within these countries—in a definite period."[73] Mao later quoted Clausewitz and Lenin in summing up his own view of the relationship between war and politics: "[P]olitics is war without bloodshed while war is politics with bloodshed."[74]

Mao had realized early on that the CCP would need its own army in order to achieve its goals. As he later emphasized, "Every Communist must grasp the truth, 'Political power grows out of the barrel of a gun.' Our principle is that the Party commands the gun, and the gun must never be allowed to command the Party."[75] Far from outlining some sort of separation of powers or system of civilian control over the military, Mao simply held that the CCP's goals could best be met by having its own army of overwhelming strength. He continued, "According to the Marxist theory of the state, the army is the chief component of state power. Whoever wants to seize and retain state power must have a strong army."[76]

In June of 1927 the Comintern cabled instructions to the CCP to form its own independent, "reliable army" of 20,000 Communists and 50,000 revolutionary workers and peasants. The same message instructed the CCP to organize a "Revolutionary Military Tribunal" to punish officers who maintained contact with Chaing Kai-shek or who "incite the soldiers against the people, the workers and peasants."[77] To implement these

13

instructions, the CCP Central Committee in August 1927 published a resolution calling for the creation of " a new revolutionary army," in which "there should be extensive political work and a party representative system, a strengthened party branch among soldiers, and dependable and loyal officers of revolution."[78] A system of Party organizations within the army was soon implemented, at four levels: Army committee, regimental committee, battalion committee, and company branch, which included a party group in each squad.[79] The army's ratio of Party members to nonparty members soon reached approximately one to three,[80] and was subsequently raised to one to two,[81] which has been maintained into the modern era.[82] During this early period, Mao repeatedly criticized those who maintained what he called "the purely military viewpoint" and emphasized the political nature of the Red army:

> [T]he Chinese Red Army is an armed body for carrying out the political tasks of the revolution. Especially at present, the Red Army should certainly not confine itself to fighting; besides fighting to destroy the enemy's military strength, it should shoulder such important tasks as doing propaganda among the masses, organizing the masses, arming them, helping them to establish revolutionary political power and setting up Party organizations. . . . Without these objectives, fighting loses its meaning and the Red Army loses the reason for its existence.[83]

One of the measures urged by Mao to correct the "military viewpoint" was the institution of what may be called, in the broad context of the CCP doctrine, a system of military law:

> Draw up Red Army rules and regulations, which clearly define its tasks, the relationship between its military and its political apparatus, the relationship between the Red Army and the masses of the people, and the powers and functions of the soldiers' committees and their relationship with the military and political organizations.[84]

Beyond a conventional system of regulations for the maintenance of military discipline, Mao called for regulation of the Army's relationship with the people and the Party. This broadened scope of military law has formed the basis of CCP doctrine to the present day. As the Revolutionary Military Tribunals ordered by the Comintern were not formally established until 1932, military discipline was maintained through informal processes within the Party committees until that time.

After the failure of the Nanching and Autumn Harvest uprisings in 1927, the remnants of the Communist insurgents took refuge in Chingkangshan, a former bandit stronghold in the mountains on the border of Hunan and Kiangsi Provinces. Here they were trained, indoctrinated and reorganized into the Chinese Workers' and Peasants' Red Army. The first rudimentary rules of discipline for the Red Army were formulated by Mao in the spring of 1928:[85]

1. Orders must be followed by action.

2. Things that belong to workers, peasants and small merchants are never touched.

3. Booty obtained from raids on local bosses[86] belongs to the public.

Six "points for attention" were developed in the summer of 1928 to ensure a good treatment of the peasantry, whose support was essential to the continued existence and development of the Red Army:

1. Put back the doors you have taken down for bed-boards.

2. Put back the straw you have used for bedding.

15

3. Speak politely.

4. Pay fairly for what you buy.

5. Return everything you borrow.

6. Pay for anything you damage.[87]

After 1929, two additional points were added:

7. Do not bathe within sight of women.

8. Do not search the pockets of captives.[88]

After several changes, and after slight variances developed in different units and areas,[89] the three rules and eight points were standardized and reissued by the General Headquarters of the Chinese Peoples' Liberation Army on 10 October 1947.[90] These remain the foundations of military discipline in the PLA, codified in Article 2 of the 1984 PLA Discipline Regulation:[91]

The Three Main Rules of Discipline

1. Obey orders in all your actions.

2. Do not take a single needle or piece of thread from the masses.

3. Turn in everything captured.

The Eight Points for Attention

1. Speak politely.

2. Pay fairly for what you buy.

3. Return everything you borrow.

4. Pay for anything you damage.

5. Do not hit or swear at people.

6. Do not damage crops.

7. Do not take liberties with women.

8. Do not ill-treat captives.

This simple code, easily memorized by even uneducated soldiers,[92] served as an educational tool illustrating two of the primary goals of the Red Army—to maintain military discipline, and to maintain good relations with the masses, whose support was essential to the Red Army concept of operations.[93] Military discipline in the Red Army thus served pragmatic political considerations as well as strictly military ones. Mao wrote in 1929: "The discipline of the Red Army is a practical propaganda to the masses. Now discipline is more lax than before; therefore it produces an unfavorable impression on the masses."[94] Mao's solution for the problem of poor discipline was simple: "The three disciplinary rules must be strictly enforced."[95]

17

Offenses more serious than violations of the disciplinary code were subject to harsh punishment in accordance with the following 1929 Red Army basic penal rules:

> 1. Wartime Discipline. Officers may shoot anyone who retreats before battle, who refuses to march forward or who otherwise disobeys orders.
>
> 2. General Discipline. Anyone who has committed any of the following crimes shall be executed: collaboration with the enemy, rebellion, defection with or without arms, rape, arson, manslaughter and fraud. Anyone resorting to gambling shall have all his money confiscated and be deprived of one month's allowance. Anyone resorting to prostitutes will be punished as if he had failed to return to his camp at night. If riots arise from prostitution, punishment in the form of death, hard labour or physical punishment will be inflicted according to the seriousness of the case. Other offenses shall be punished according to their nature.[96]

D.   Military Law in the Chinese Soviet Republic (1931-1934)

On 7 November 1931 the CCP proclaimed its own government for the mostly rural and impoverished areas it controlled—the Chinese Soviet Republic (CSR). Before it was crushed by the Nationalist government in 1934, the CSR had developed a considerable body of law. Despite the nearly constant warfare with the counterrevolutionaries within the CSR areas and the Nationalists without, foundations for a rather elaborate legal structure were laid. Statutes were enacted to provide for a system of courts, land and labor laws, a marriage law, even a "statute on investment of capital in industrial and trade enterprises."[97] Much of the experience gained during the CSR period is reflected in the legal system established after 1949 in the People's Republic of China.

At the First All-China Congress of Soviets in November 1931, Mao's concept of a thoroughly politicized Red Army was reemphasized. The Congress proclaimed the Chinese Workers' and Peasants' Red Army to be "a political army ... of class-conscious warriors," in which "the strictest and most conscious revolutionary discipline must prevail," and that "the organizations of the Communist Party and the Young Communist League are inalienable, integral parts of the Red Army."[98] The class nature of the Red Army was made clear: only workers, peasants, and the urban poor could join. Members of "the ruling or exploiting class" (militarists, landlords, gentry, bureaucrats, capitalists, rich peasants and members of their families) were not permitted.[99] As incentives for enlisting, and to improve morale, certain benefits and privileges were extended to Red Army soldiers and their families, such as land allotments, tax exemptions and survivor benefits.[100] Failure to carry out these privileges was punishable as a counterrevolutionary crime.[101]

The role of the developing military legal system during the CSR period was not limited to maintaining internal discipline in the Red Army. The Red Army Military Courts were an integral part of the broader tasks of the CSR legal system: "the establishment of revolutionary order and protection of the rights of the people's masses."[102] As is evident from the title of the first CSR directive establishing a judicial system, the "Provisional Procedure for Deciding Cases on Counter-Revolutionary Crimes and Instituting Judicial Organs," the preeminent thrust of this system was the suppression of "counterrevolutionaries."[103] Two of the major instruments used by the CCP for this task were the State Political Security Bureau (SPSB) and the military tribunals of the Red Army. The SPSB was established as the CCP's own secret service in 1928, patterned after the Soviet GPU.[104] It was authorized to investigate and file accusations in counterrevolutionary cases, while trial and judgment were formally reserved to state judicial organs (to include those of the Red

Army).[105]   However, since the SPSB was authorized to try and execute counterrevolutionaries during the period of civil war and Soviet expansion,[106] its powers were virtually absolute. SPSB sections were to be established within the Red Army at corps and division level; agents could be assigned to lower echelons as well.[107] The Red Army was required to maintain a close relationship with the SPSB in order to concentrate on purging "bad elements" and liquidating counterrevolutionary activities, and to place units at the disposal of the SPSB when necessary.[108]

Red Army military tribunals were formalized on 1 February 1932 when the Central Executive Committee (CEC) of the CSR promulgated the "Provisional Organizational Regulations for Military Courts of the Chinese Soviet Republic."[109] These regulations, although in force for only a short period, established models for the Chinese Communist military legal system which have continued, in many respects, to the present day.[110] Four types of military courts were to be established at three levels: primary and primary field military courts, in echelons down to division level; a superior military court for the entire Red Army; and, as a tribunal of last resort, the Supreme Military Judicial Conference, to be established within the Supreme Court.[111]

The jurisdiction of the military courts extended beyond the members of the Red Army to include residents of battle zones.[112] The courts could punish violations of "the criminal law, the military criminal law, or some other law," as well as espionage cases.[113] However, cases involving "violations of common discipline but not of the law" were specifically excluded from the courts' jurisdiction.[114]

Military trial courts were to be composed of one judge and two elected assessors.[115] Appellate and reviewing courts were to be composed of a presiding judge and two panel judges.[116] Verdicts could be appealed to the next higher level court,[117] and death sentences were to be reviewed by the next higher court, whether appealed or not.[118]

The Regulations also established the Military Procuracy. Military procurators were empowered to conduct preliminary investigations, bring cases before the military courts, and represent the state at trial.[119] Primary and superior military procuracies were established and attached to the military courts of the respective level.[120]

The February 1932 military courts statute, together with its civilian counterpart adopted in June,[121] marked the peak of the trend toward the normalization of judicial procedure and restricting the power of the SPSB. Thereafter, in view of the worsening military situation with the KMT, attitudes toward procedural safeguards for the accused hardened, and differentiation between the military and civilian legal systems deteriorated.

The Central Executive Committee (CEC) reemphasized the class struggle in its Directive 21 of 15 March 1933 "On the Question of Suppressing Internal Counterrevolution,"[122] which called for strict attention on the part of government organizations at all levels to suppressing counterrevolutionaries. "Resolute and rapid measures must be taken to repress them severely," it warned. Proclamations of a temporary state of martial law were authorized "when the situation is pressing." Judicial organs were ordered to deal quickly with counterrevolutionary cases: "all elements whose crimes have been clearly proven, starting with the alien class elements among them, must immediately be put to death." Directive 21 also suspended Article 26 of the civilian court regulations, which had required review by higher courts before executing death sentences,[123] and allowed: "death sentences may be carried out first and the cases reported to superiors afterward."

21

The increasingly difficult situation produced two additional problems for the CCP: runaways from the Soviet areas, and deserters from the Red Army. To control runaways, strict controls were placed on allowing people to leave the Soviet areas. Only persons "who are determined to have a need to go outside the area" were permitted to depart. "They must be subjected to close examination and not allowed to leave the area at will."[124] An exit visa specifying the departure route and a travel pass, both issued by the SPSB, were required. Mass meetings were employed to encourage runaways to go home, and relatives and friends were pressured to urge runaways to return. The Red Army and other government organizations were ordered to cooperate with the SPSB "in order to intensify the Red martial law."

Desertion from the Red Army became a severe problem. In a five-month period of 1933, the First Army Corps had 203 deserters, the Third Army 98, and the Fifth Army 110.[125] In one area, 80% of the troops ran away.[126] "Class deviates" within the Red Army, as well as incorrect and coercive leadership by officers, were cited as explanations for the high desertion rates.[127] Other factors included dissatisfaction among forced conscripts, and difficult living conditions at the front. In response to the desertion problem, the CCP organized campaigns within its "Enlarging the Red Army Movement." A propaganda campaign promising lenient treatment was directed at winning back the majority of the deserters, while harsh punishments were given to leaders and repeat offenders.

A uniform procedure to deal with the desertion problem was promulgated in CEC Order Number 25 on 15 December 1933.[128] Soldiers who deserted with their rifles were to be summarily shot upon apprehension. Leaders and organizers of desertion were to be executed after being made examples at mass trials. Repeat offenders were to be tried by the military courts and could be sentenced to penal servitude or death. However, individual deserters who went home (without their weapons) "for lack of political consciciousness" were to be subjected to "propaganda and agitation" while their families continued to receive the preferential treatment due the families of Red Army men in general,[129] "so that they will return to the army of their own free will." Those who still refused to return were required to indemnify the state for any clothing, supplies or family assistance they had received. Harboring deserters was prohibited. Those who failed to carry out this order were to be dealt with as having aided and abetted desertion and undermined the Red Army.

A typical mass trial of deserters took place on 26 April 1933 in Jui-chang hsien (county).[130] Representatives from over 30 hsien and from 80 Model Regiments attended. An agent of the SPSB served as procurator, presenting the evidence against two counterrevolutionary Social Democrats, and two poor peasants who had sincerely confessed their mistakes. After the various representatives spoke out in turn against the evils of desertion, the crowd demanded death for the two Social Democrats, who were shot after being paraded through the town. The two peasants were sentenced to hard labor, one to a long term, and the other to one year.

From the fall of 1933 through 1934 the CSR was threatened by the KMT's Fifth Encirclement Campaign. A new strategy of military and economic blockade, on the advice of German advisors, was proving to be more successful than previous KMT assaults. In response to the increased KMT threat, the CCP adopted more drastic measures in a climate of lessened legal restraints. The new chairman of the Council of People's Commissars, Chang Wen-t'ien, complained that the judicial system was applying the soviet laws incorrectly and too leniently in counterrevolutionary cases.[131] In February 1934 the SPSB in Red Army units and local governments was formally authorized to arrest, try and even execute spies and counterrevolutionaries without going through the military or local courts. Executions were to be subsequently reported to the Central SPSB. If military or local government officials disagreed with an SPSB death sentence, the sentence was to be carried out anyway, and the Council of People's Commissars would "determine whether the punishment was right or wrong."[132]

Criticism of the legal system increased. Liang Po-t'ai, the Commissar of Justice, complained in his article of 1 March 1934 in Hung-se Chung-hua (Red China) that judicial cadres did not understand that "the laws are developing in accordance with the demands of the revolution."[133] He continued: "What is to the advantage of the revolution, that is the law. Whenever it is to the advantage of the revolution the legal procedure can at any time be adapted. One ought not to hinder the interests of the revolution because of legal procedure."

The trend toward a more radical legal system culminated on 8 April 1934 when the CEC promulgated the "Judicial Procedure of the CSR"[134] and the "Statute of the CSR Governing the Punishment of Counterrevolutionaries."[135] These two statutes would govern the operation of the legal system until the fall of the CSR in October 1934.

In the Judicial Procedure the CSR abandoned its previous tentative steps toward a regularized and differentiated legal system, with a separate military legal system having jurisdiction only over military personnel. Article 8 of the Judicial Procedure rescinded the military court statute of 1 February 1932, along with the civilian courts statute of 9 June 1932 and the provisional judicial procedure of 13 December 1931. The military courts were now granted a concurrent sweeping jurisdiction to apprehend, try, sentence and execute "all criminals."[136] The board powers earlier granted the SPSB in Decree 5 were confirmed. The system of automatic confirmation of judgments by higher courts was abolished.[137] In its place was granted a right to appeal to the next higher court within seven days. Counterrevolutionaries, landlords and gentry were denied appellate rights in border areas, areas under attack and in "critical situations." The sole procedural guarantee estabished was a two-level system of preliminary hearings and final trials.[138] A preliminary hearing at a primary military court was to culminate in a final trial at the next higher level military court. However, no appeal was to be allowed after decision under this two-level system, unless the procurator was dissatisfied with the decision.

The Statute on Punishing Counterrevolutionaries further reflects the deterioration of the distinction between civilian and military law as military offenses were intermingled with civilian crimes in one statute of general application. Soldiers surrendering to the enemy with their weapons or other military equipment, or who persuaded others to surrender, were to be executed.[139] The provisions of the December 1933 AWOL order were incorporated into Article 18, which prescribes the death penalty for Red Army members who organize or lead desertion, or who individually desert the Red Army five or more times. Other military-related crimes included were: destroying, abandoning or selling military materiel; disobeying orders "with a counterrevolutionary purpose," or otherwise creating confusion at the front; murdering "the revolutionary masses," stealing or destroying their property, or otherwise damaging "the prestige of the Soviet and the Red Army among the masses"; revealing state or military secrets; and making or possessing "counterrevolutionary propaganda" material.[140]

25

Evaluation of the CSR Period

The Chinese Communist military legal system underwent considerable development during the CSR period. Although its jurisdiction was enlarged to include civilians in a virtual state of martial law during the last year of the CSR, the basic norms of a differentiated military legal system with jurisdiction essentially limited to military members were in place by 1932. The military courts system was the first judicial organization to be formalized in the CSR and the first to embody many of the Soviet model features that would become typical in the PRC, including the procuracy, lay assessors, and the collegial bench.

a. Preference for Informal Adjudication

The operation of the military courts reflected the traditional Chinese preference for resolving conflicts at a lower level whenever possible. Since Red Army members were by definition members of the favored classes, their transgressions were to be handled leniently. Breaches of military discipline were kept out of the military courts, where only grave breaches of law and counterrevolutionary crimes were to be punished. Until the Statute on Punishing Counterrevolutionaries was enacted in 1934, military courts had only the military's own early basic laws and disciplinary codes, along with several Party and CSR orders or directives, to apply. Once a case was brought to court a guilty verdict could routinely be expected, since the procurators and the SPSB would have already thoroughly investigated and rendered a preliminary decision. In cases of great importance, usually involving counterrevolutionaries, mass trials were employed.

b.   Subordination of law to state policy

The traditional Chinese subordination of law to the dominant state philosophy was also apparent during the CSR period. The political goals of the CSR legal system were to establish revolutionary order and protect the rights of "the people's masses."[141] However, as a "democratic dictatorship of the proletariat and peasantry,"[142] equality before the law applied only to "workers, peasants, Red Army soldiers, and all toilers and their families."[143]   The CSR denied rights of citizenship to "militarists, bureaucrats, landlords, the gentry, village bosses, monks [and] all exploiting and counter-revolutionary elements."[144]   This discrimination of legal treatment based on class was evident in many CSR legal enactments. For example, CEC Order Number 6 (December 1931)[145] prescribed heavy punishments for counterrevolutionary elements from landlord-gentry, rich peasant and capitalist backgrounds, as well as for ringleaders. However, members of counterrevolutionary organizations recruited from the ranks of workers, peasants, and the toiling masses were to receive "light judgments."

A similar provision appears in Article 11 of the Organic Program of the SPSB. Punishment was to be "defined by the class line."[146] Workers, peasants and Red Army members who participated in counterrevolutionary activities as mere followers were to be leniently treated, through reprimands, detention, dismissal from the military or loss of civil rights. Offenders from the enemy classes would be punished severely.

The 1934 Statute on Punishing Counterrevolutionaries also provided lighter penalties for crimes committed by workers, peasants, or individuals who had rendered meritorious services to the Soviet.[147] Under the Judicial Procedure, "local magnates and landlords" were deprived of their right to appeal court decision.[148] The class-oriented approach to justice in the

27

CSR was summed up by Mao Tse-tung in his report to the Second All-China Congress of Soviets in January 1934: "The objective of the Soviet courts is the suppression of crimes committed by the landlord bourgeoisie, and sentences meted out are generally light on crimes committed by worker-peasant elements.... [T]he Soviet courts severely suppressed the activities of the counterrevolutionary elements, and the Soviet should not display any leniency whatsoever toward such elements."[149] Since Red Army members were by definition included among the favored classes (indeed, members of bad classes could not enlist), these class provisions were advantageous. They reinforced the tendency to maximize administrative handling of transgressions, leaving most Red Armymen's disciplinary offenses outside the jurisdiction of the military courts.

c.   Voluntary surrender and confession

The Chinese tradition of extending leniency toward offenders who voluntarily surrendered and confessed their crimes was incorporated into the CSR legal system. However, the CSR went still further, granting leniency to those who, after detection of their offenses, "repented" and aided the authorities by exposing co-conspirators.[150]

d.   Analogy

Article 38 of the Statute on Punishing Counterrevoluntaries provided for punishment of crimes not specified in the statute by application of analogy: "Any counterrevolutionary criminal behavior not included in this statute shall be punished according to the article in this statute dealing with similar crimes."

The incorporation of the principle of analogy in CSR law was both rooted in traditional Chinese law, and derived from the laws of the Soviet

Union. Application of criminal statutes by analogy was allowed under the imperial codes, but was abolished in the codes of the ROC.[151] In Russia, analogy had been included in the early Tsarist codes, until its abolition in the 1903 code revision.[152] After the Bolshevik seizure of power, there being relatively few legal rules, tribunals were to rely on the application of "revolutionary communist legal consciousness."[153] When the Soviet codes were eventually established, analogy was restored in order to fill any gaps in the laws.[154]

E.   The "United Front" Period

On October 16, 1934, 90,000 Red Army members broke through the Nationalist armies encircling the CSR area and began the "long march," ostensibly "to fight Japan in the North."[155] Thirteen months and over 6,000 miles later, fewer than 20,000 survivors were attempting to rebuild their forces in their barren new base, Yenan, in nothern Shensi province. To avoid destruction by a final KMT extermination campaign, the CCP skillfully sought to take advantage of public opinion to force a "united front" with the Nationalist government against Japan. After the Sino-Japanese War broke out in July 1937, the CCP Central Committee made four public pledges in connection with the newly-concluded united front: (1) to abide by Sun Yat-sen's Three People's Principles (nationalism, democracy, people's livelihood); (2) that the CCP "abandons all its policy of overthrowing the KMT by force and the movement of sovietization, and discontinues its policy of forcible confiscation of land from landlords"; (3) that the CCP's "Soviet government" would be abolished and the nation unified; and (4) that the Red Army would be abolished and its troops reorganized into the national army under the control of the National Government.[156] In contrast with its public propaganda of cooperation, the CCP privately planned to utilize the critical wartime situation to implement Mao's policy of "70 per cent expansion, 20 per cent dealing with the Kuomintang, and 10 per cent resisting Japan."[157] Mao outline a three-stage United Front strategy to his military cadres: first, a compromising stage to safeguard the CCP's existence and development; second, a struggle phase to build CCP political and military strength; and third, an offensive stage to seize power.[158]

The CCP consolidated its rule in the Shensi-Kansu-Ninghsia Border Region, the Shansi-Chahar-Hopei Border Region, and other areas which remained the bases of CCP operations throughout the Second World War. During this period the military legal foundations laid and subsequently abandoned during the Chinese Soviet Republic and reestablished and developed. The Red Army was renamed the Eighth Route Army, and the courts were nominally under the jurisdiction of the National Supreme Court. In reality, the judicial systems of the Eighth Route Army and of each border region operated as separate entities.

During the period the military legal system further developed its dual function of maintaining military discipline and furthering the political objectives of the CCP. In 1937, Mao outlined three basic principles of political work within the Eighth Route Army which illustrate the political role of the military legal system:

> First, the principle of unity between officers and men, which means eradicating feudal practices in the army, prohibiting beating and abuse, buidling up a conscious discipline, and sharing weal and woe—as a result of which the entire army is closely united. Second, the principle of unity between the army and the people, which means maintaining a discpline that forbids the slightest violation of the people's interests, conducting propaganda among the masses, organizing and arming them, lightening their economic burdens and suppressing the traitors and collaborators who do harm to the army and the people—as a result of which the army is closely united with the people and welcomed everywhere. Third, the principle of disintegrating the enemy troops and giving

lenient treatment to prisoners of war. Our victory depends not only upon our military operations but also upon the disintegration of the enemy troops.[159]

In February 1938, the Shansi-Chahar-Hopei (SCH) Border Region government reissued a 1937 ROC statute on "Emergency Crimes Endangering the Republic."[160] While the exigencies of war and martial law are reflected in the extension of military jurisdiction over a lengthy list of offenses committed "for the purpose of endangering the Republic," some important refinements in the legal system, previously abandoned by the CSR, were reestablished. Article 8 provides that military tribunals must report their decisions, together with the facts of the case tried, "to their superior organ of military justice for approval prior to implementation." Article 9 further rquires military or police organs to immediately notify their governing organs of all arrests made. Cases not covered by this emergency statute were to be handled under the provisions of the criminal law of the ROC (Article 10).

In October 1938 the SCH border region government promulgated its own separate Revised Statute Concerning Punishment of Traitors.[161] In many respects similar to the CSR statute on counterrevolutionaries, the SCH statute reflects the different conditions of the United Front in that the traitors were no longer the "counterrevolutionaries," but were now defined as those who cooperated with an enemy country. Like the 1937 ROC statute, the SCH border region statute provides for military jurisdiction over a lengthy list of offenses committed to help "the enemy," such as selling him materiel and food; disclosing information concerning the military, political or economic situation; sabotage; and currency offenses (Article 14). While the earlier statute on emergency crimes provided for review only by the next higher organ of military justice, the October statute required a summary of the decision, together with the evidence and the defense offered, to be sent to the highest organ of military affairs of the central government for decision (Article 15). The highest military organ could then choose among four courses of action: (1) approve the decision, (2) transfer the case to other organs, (3) send new personnel to retry the case, or (4) re-try the case itself. Article 5 severely discouraged false accusations: "Those who falsely accuse others of any crime under this statute should be punished according to that article."

Further differentiation between military and civilian jurisdiction was reestablished in the 1939 Shensi-Kansu-Ninghsia (SKN) Border Region "Martial Law."[162] Military jurisdiction was limited under the statute to those civilians committing one of the enumerated, mostly military-related crimes within a war zone or contiguous area when martial law was in effect. Even in these cases the military judicial organs had the option of transferring the case to the civilian courts for trial (Article 5). A requirement that appropriate compensation be made for destroyed or requisitioned property in martial law areas further demonstrates the role of military law as a means of maintaining popular support for the army (Articles 6 and 7). Additional evidence of this policy is seen in the 1939 SKN border region statute "Governing Punishment of Traitors in Wartime,"[163] which made burning and looting capital offenses (Article 3).

The separation of the military and civilian legal systems was reinforced by the 1942 SKN "Statute Protecting Human and Property Rights,"[164] enacted at the height of the United Front period. The statute provided that "except in periods of martial law, nonmilitary personnel who commit crimes will not be tried by military law" (Article 13). The statute provided for a number of additional procedural safeguards, for both the military and civilian legal systems. The right to appeal was allowed (Article 18). Cases involving the death penalty were to be reviewed and approved by the central border region government before execution, even if no appeal was filed, although emergency wartime situations could be exempted from this requirement (Article 19). Arrested persons and any evidence were to be presented to the procurator or the Public Security Bureau within 24 hours of the arrest (Article 9), and judicial organs were to decide the case within 30 days of receiving it (Article 11).

Military trials during this period were conducted publicly and followed a rather informal procedure, as might be expected in a wartime situation:

> While the masses did not yell and shout slogans, as in the mass trials, they were free to question the criminal during the proceedings. The defendant and witnesses testified and the judge questioned them. Agnes Smedley describes the chief judge of one such court as a young officer with five years of regular schooling. His chief education had been in the army. She says, "Of ordinary law he knew nothing, but he knew patriots, he knew traitors, and he knew politicians who would be traitors if they could."[165]

By the end of this period the Chinese Communist military legal system had undergone considerable substantive and procedural development. While retaining the role of regulating internal military discipline, the military legal system was functionally differentiated from the civilian system as its jurisdiction over civilians and civilian offenses was progressively limited.

IV. DEVELOPMENT OF MILITARY LAW IN THE PEOPLE'S REPUBLIC OF CHINA

A. Period of Consolidation (1949-1953)

As the second world war ended, the long-standing bitter rivalry between the CCP and KMT reached a climax which resulted in renewed civil war and the triumph of Communist power throughout all of mainland China. During this period of struggle and rapid expansion, the military

33

legal system was again called upon to enlarge the scope of its jurisdiction to include the civilian sector. As areas came under Communist control, the administrative and legal functions were assumed by the military.

In February 1949 the Central Committee of the CCP issued a directive abrogating the legal codes of the ROC and prescribing the judicial principles to be applied in the "liberated areas." "Work of the people's judiciary," it stated, "should not be based on the Kuomintang's Six Codes but should be based on new people's laws."[166] While a unified system of laws was lacking in the communist areas, regional and party directives or regulations provided some form of legal order. Since no comprehensive military codes were introduced to replace those of the KMT, various military units maintained their own separate disciplinary regulations.[167]

On the eve of the proclamation of the PRC, a provisional constitution was adopted. This "Common Program,"[168] in accordance with the policy of the CCP, delcared the complete abolition of the laws and courts of the Nationalist government: "All laws, decrees and judicial systems of the Kuomintang reactionary government which oppress the people shall be abolished. Laws and decrees protecting the people shall be enacted and the people's judicial system shall be established" (Article 17). The Common Program further provided that the PLA should establish Military Control Committees as the governing organs in all newly-liberated areas, to "lead the people in establishing revolutionary order and suppressing counter-revolutionary activities" (Article 14). The military control committees and their military tribunals were to exercise administrative and legal authority during the period of consolidation and reorganization until elections could be held and the local People's Governments could assume power.

The role and functions of the military tribunals during the early part of this transitionary period are illustrated by the case of Wang Kuo-jui, a

PLA truck driver in Shanghai.[169]   On 3 June 1949, shortly after the Communist takeover of Shanghai, Wang was speeding in his army truck when he struck and killed a bicycling university student. The Political Department of the Shanghai Garrison Headquarters investigated the case, and Wang admitted his guilt. The Judge Advocate Division of the Political Department quickly imposed a death sentence "in order to enforce our army's strict discipline," and "as a warning to furture careless drivers," which was announced in the press on 6 June 1949. No law or regulation was cited as the basis for the crime or sentence. The sentence elicited appeals for clemency from the public. The case was submitted for review to the Commander, Policial Commissar and Deputy Commander of the East China Military District, and the following order was announced:

> Driver Wang Kuo-jui, who caused the death of a person while operating a vehicle against police regulations, should receive the death penalty. However, many people of the working class and educational and business communities have earnestly appealed by mail or telegraph for a commutation so that the culprit, Wang, may have a chance to redeem himself through meritorious service. Respectful of public opinion, this headquarters hereby commutes the death penalty to three years penal servitude.[170]

The case shows the dominant operational role of the policial authorities in investigating, adjudicating and reviewing the case. Besides keeping order and demonstrating their strict military discipline, the new communist regime also educated the masses by first imposing the death sentence as an example and then commuting it "in respect of public opinion," in accordance with the long-standing policy of seeking the support of the people.

During this period of consolidation the PRC gradually filled the void left by the complete abrogation of all the Nationalist codes by enacting statutes governing specific crimes, such as the Statute on Penalties for

Corruption,[171] and the Statute on Punishment for Counterrevolutionary Activity.[172] As had been the case during the CSR period, the legal system was mainly directed at suppressing "counterrevolutionaries."

The Statute on Punishing Counterrevolutionaries contained numerous enumerated counterrevolutionary offenses, as well as two broad articles to cover almost any eventuality. Article 18 made the act retroactive to cover offenses committed before the establishment of the PRC, and Article 16 adopted the traditional principle of analogy: "Persons who have committed other crimes for counterrevolutionary purposes that are not specified in this Statute are subject to the punishment applicable to the crimes which most closely resemble those specified in this Statute." Additionally, the 1951 Provisional Regulations for the Preservation of State Secrets further expanded the scope of counterrevolutionary offenses by adopting sweeping and vague definitions of what constitutes state secrets, to include almost anything not publicly released, as well as the catch-all phrase "other state affairs that must be kept secret."[173] In nationwide mass campaigns such as the Land Reform and Suppression of Counterrevolutionaries movements, military tribunals and ad hoc people's tribunals[174] conducted mass trials and condemned millions to death or long-term "reform through labor."[175] Mao called for stern measures to be taken against counterrevolutionaries, to include abrogation of the traditional practice of "suspending a [death] sentence for two years."[176] However, for those "counterrevolutionaries" purged from the Party, Government and PLA, a more lenient line was adopted:

> [G]enerally it is necessary to exercise the principle of imposing the capital punishment on 10 - 20 percent of them and adopt the policy of passing the death sentence on the rest, then placing them on probation with forced labor, and watching over the counsquences. In this way, we will be able to gain the sympathy of society, avoid mistakes on our part in regard to this problem, and split up and disintegrate our

enemies. This will be advantageous in utterly destroying the counterrevolutionary force, and preserve a big labor force, which will be beneficial to national production and construction.[177]

The military tribunals often administered civilian as well as military cases during this period. In June 1950 the Military Tribunal of the Peking Municipal Military Control Committee announced several death sentences in espionage and robbery cases.[178] As late as August 1951 the same Military Tribunal announced the decision of 418 cases concerning counterrevolutionary offenses.[179] Military jurisdiction over civilians accused of counterrevolutionary activity was limited by the 1951 statute on counterrevolutionaries to those periods when military control committees were functioning.[180] It should also be noted that the 1951 statute does not intermingle civilian with strictly military offenses, as did the 1934 CSR statute on counterrevolutionaries. Thus the military and civilian legal systems were clearly separate by this time, even though provision was made for extending military jurisdiction over the civilian system during times of crisis.

The operation of military tribunals in trying civilians under the 1951 Statute on Punishing Counterrevolutionaries is illustrated by an espionage case decided 17 August 1951 by the military court of the Peking Military Control Committee.[181] Lo Jui-ching, Procurator General of the Peking Municipal Peoples Procurator's office, charged seven defendants of various nationalities with "conspiracy to armed assault, concealing arms and ammunition, and spying out secrets of the Chinese State," under the direction of the United States.[182] There was no provision for defense, and the defendants were not represented by defense counsel. The Public Security Bureau had already investigated and "proved with conclusive evidence" the guilt of the accused. Typically, all the defendants confessed their guilt. The military court found all the defendants guilty of violating various articles of the Statute on Punishment for Counterrevolutionary Activity. In accordance with Article 18 of the statute, the court applied the statute retroactively, as all of the crimes were committed before the statute was enacted on 20 February 1951. Indeed, five of the seven defendants had been in custody since 26 September 1950. The court was careful to cite Article 20 of the statute as the legal basis for its jurisdiction over the civilian defendants, as the period of military control had not yet ended in Peking.[183] Two of the defendants were sentenced to death, and the others to terms of imprisonment ranging from five years to life. Evidently no appeal was allowed, as the two death sentences were executed on the day the verdict was pronounced.[184]

B.   "Constitutional" Period (1954-1965)

During the early years of the Constitutional period, there was a clear ascendancy of the more formalized "jural" model of justice over the informal "societal" model which had prevailed during the period of consolidation. The Constitution[185] promulgated on 20 September 1954 reflected a new effort to achieve a regularized and institutionalized system. Like the 1936 Constitution of the USSR,[186] the PRC Constitution promised that courts would be independent and subject only to the law (Article 78), and that all citizens were "equal before the law" (Article 85). Citizenship, however, was not universal: "The state deprives feudal landlords and bureaucrat-capitalists of political rights for a specific period of time according to law" (Article 19). Nevertheless, the legal system was regularized to such an extent that a preeminent Chinese legal text could declare: "Judicial organs can only impose punishment on the basis of the law and in accordance with the seriousness and size of the crimes and the attitude and behavior of the criminal. It is not permissible to handle matters not in accordance with the law."[187]

The military was also regularized under the 1954 Constitution. The armed forces of the CCP, having achieved the seizure of national power, and having learned from the experiences of the Korean war, now assumed the role of a national force. The state, rather than the Party, was now to control the armed forces, with the PRC chairman as commander in chief (Article 42). A regular officer corps[188] and a system of national conscription[189] were also introduced.

A separate formal system of military courts was established by the 1954 Constitution and the organic laws enacted under its authority. Besides establishing a Supreme People's Court and local people's courts, the Constitution provided for military courts as part of a system of "special courts" (Article 73). The Organic Law of the People's Courts,[190] adopted one day after the Constitution was proclaimed, specified the establishment of military courts as one of the special courts (Article 26). Military procuracies were also authorized under the provision for special peoples procuracies of the Organic Law of the People's Procuratorates.[191] While both statutes specified that the organization of military courts and procuracies would be prescribed separately by the National People's Congress,[192] no such acts have been published in the official "Collection of Laws and Regulations of the People's Republic of China."[193] If enacted, these organizational regulations probably were classified under the broad 1951 Regulation for the Preservation of State Secrets.

Military courts and procuracies were established at all levels in September 1954.[194] Their function during this period was described in a later New China News Agency report:

> Under the leadership of party committees and political organs at various levels, the military legal organs cooperated with and exercised a check-and-balance with the security department, enforced and protected the law, dealt effective

blows to sabotage activities of class enemies at home and abroad, protected the legitimate rights and interests of all PLA commanders and fighters, and purified the PLA ranks. They played a role in strengthening the army and insuring the successful execution of battle plans and various tasks.[195]

The highest organ of military law was the Military Division of the Supreme Peoples' Court. The Military Division had a status equal to the Court's three general divisions (two criminal and one civil).[196] The chief judge of the Military Division was concurrently a member of the judicial committee of the Supreme People's Court.[197]

Military courts were organized in each of the country's eleven Military Regions and at the Military Provincial District level.[198] The military courts tried cases involving "contradictions between ourselves and the enemy or criminal elements who violate criminal law."[199] A functionally specialized class of Judge Advocate officers to carry out legal duties was provided in the Regulations on the Service of Officers.[200]

In the absence of a unified PRC criminal code or a military criminal code, the military courts initially applied a series of separate regulations such as the "PLA Provisional Military Regulation for Eastern China" or the "Provisional military law and discipline of the 9th corps of the Chinese People's Volunteers in time of war."[201] PRC statutes governing specific crimes were also applied.[202] In 1963 a unified military discipline regulation was issued, followed by an internal administration regulation in 1964.[203] As there was no known military procedural code or guide equivalent to the U.S. Manual for Courts-Martial, the military courts generally followed principles and procedures similar to those of the civilian court system.[204]

The operation of the higher military courts during this period is illustrated by two related espionage cases decided by the Military Tribunal of the Supreme People's Court on 23 September 1954.[205] The Tribunal was composed of Chief Judge Chia Chien and Judges Chu Yao-tang and Chang Hsiang-chien.

In the first case the Military Procurator of the Supreme People's Procuratorate filed charges of espionage against eleven U.S. airmen (ranging in rank from Colonel to Corporal) whose B-29 had been shot down over China near North Korea on 12 January 1953. Significantly, no mention is made of the defendants making the customary admissions of guilt, although two of the accused apparently revealed some incriminating information. Nevertheless, all were found guilty of espionage and reconnaissance activity, as well as attempting to "resupply and maintain liaison with other U.S. special agents," in violation of Articles 6, 11, and 16 of the Statute on Punishing Counterrevolutionaries. The U.S. wing commander was sentenced to 10 years' imprisonment; the operations officer received a "lightended" sentence of eight years since he had "shown repentance" during the investigations and trial. The pilot was sentenced to six years' imprisonment, and the crew members were given "mitigated sentences" of five or four years because they did not bear the "main responsibility."

In the second case, two U.S. civilians and nine Chinese nationals ("former military officers of the Chiang Kai-shek gang") were accused of espionage and, on the part of the Chinese, high treason. The indictment alleged that the nine Chinese defendants had been parachuted into China in July, September, and October 1952. The two American were captured when their plane was shot down on 29 November, in an attempt to contact and resupply the nine Chinese defendants. In accordance with the traditional Chinese practice of confession, all the defendants "admitted the crimes committed by them." Under articles 6, 3, 7, 11, 14 and 16 of the Statute on Punishing Counterrevolutionaries, the two Americans were

41

sentenced to terms of life and twenty years' imprisonment, respectively. Four of the Chinese defendants were sentenced to death. Another four were "given lighter sentences" of life imprisonment because they had "shown repentance during the trial." One defendant, having "shown true repentance during the trial," was given a "mitigated sentence" of fifteen years' imprisonment.

These two cases reflect the institutionalization and regularization of the military court system achieved during the Constitutional period. In contrast with the previously-considered 1951 espionage case decided by the Military Tribunal of the Peking Military Control Committee,[206] the 1954 cases were heard at the highest level of a fully established system of military courts. While the 1951 case had been prosecuted by the Peking Municipal Procuratorate, the state was represented in the 1954 cases by the Military Procurator of the Supreme People's Procuratorate. Significantly, defense counsel were appointed to represent the defendants in the 1954 cases; no defense counsel had been provided in the 1951 case.[207] However, the Military Tribunal of the Supreme People's Court never addressed the source of its jurisdiction over the defendants in the 1954 case, none of whom were members of the PLA. The 1951 cases had cited as its souce of jurisdiction Article 20 of the statute on punishing counterrevolutionaries, which permitted civilians to be tried by military tribunals while military control committees were administering the civil government. As military administration was no longer in effect in 1954, the jurisdictional basis for these cases is unclear.

Even as the 1954 cases demonstrate the modernization and regularization of the military court system, they also reveal several characteristic features retained from the traditional Chinese and early Communist judicial systems. First, the traditional penchant for procuring confessions is evident. The related traditional practice of granting leniency for repentance shown after confession is also retained.[208] Finally, the court applied the traditional principle of analogy by citing the analogy article of the Statute on Punishing Counterrevolutionaries as one of the bases for its judgment.[209]

Cases of lesser gravity involving breaches of miltiary discipline or minor criminal offenses were generally handled administratively within local military units. Reflecting the dominant role of the Communist Party in military affairs, the administration of military discipline was a joint responsibility of the commander and the unit political commissar. Party committees, supervised by the commissar, are organized at each level of the PLA, "to serve as the nucleus of unified leadership and solidarity in the Army units. . . . All important issues . . . must be referred to the Party committees for discussion and decision." The commander and the commissar are both "the leading officers of the Army units, jointly responsible for the Army's work."[210] The commissars have authority over prevention of desertion or dereliction of duty, investigation and complaints, discipline, and the handling of prisoners of war.[211]

C. Cultural Revolution Period (1966-1976)

The regularization of the military legal system, as well as its clear differentation from the civilian system, virtually disappeared during the Cultural Revolution. Once again, as had been the case during the earlier civil war periods, military jurisdiction was extended to include the civilian sector during this new time of crisis.

The ascendancy of the jural model during the Constitutional Period was short-lived. Even before the Cultural Revolution was launched, the process of regularization of the legal system had given way to a rising tide of radicalism. The preeminence of law proclaimed in the 1954 Constitution and 1954 Lectures on Criminal law was superseded by a more Maoist doctrine explained in an article written by the Department of Law of the People's University of China: "Every aspect of our legal work must be placed under the absolute leadership of the Communist Party," whose policy "is not only the basis of law making, it is also the basis of law execution."[212] The legal system must "combine principle with flexibility" so as to be responsive to "the permanent revolution in society."[213] Flexibility would also be better served by less precison in the laws: "Some people think that the more detailed the law, the better it is. This is an impractical idea."[214]

Mao Tse-tung launched the Cultural Revolution in 1966, in an attempt to regain political dominance and impose Maoist norms on society. Hoardes of youthful Red Guards were unleashed, zealously attacking the existing state and party power structure under the slogan of "continuing revolution." Tremendous disruption resulted; hundreds of thousands were persecuted, and many were killed.[215]

The formal legal system was a particular target of the Maoists. On 31 January 1967 the People's Daily printed an editorial entitled "In Praise of Lawlessness,"[216] calling for the complete destruction of the "bourgeois" law so that a more "proletarian" law could be established. The Red Guards denounced the 1954 organic laws of the courts and procuracies and the entire structure of "legal procedure, judicial proceedings, etc." as "feudal, capitalist, and revisionist."[217] The concepts of "everyone is equal before the law," "presumption of innocence," and representation by defense counsel were condemned.[218] Independent administration of justice was termed a "poisonous weed."[219] Quoting Mao as instructing, "Depend on the rule of man, not the rule of law," the Red Guards proclaimed that "our carrying out work according to Chairman Mao's instruction is the highest criterion in the execution of law."[220] Following Mao's 1967 instruction to "smash Kung-chien-fa" (police procuracy and courts),[221] the courts and public security organs were severely disrupted, and the procuracy was abolished entirely.[222]

Mao's ally Lin Piao, head of the PLA, soon ordered the army into the conflict to support the Maoist faction. The CCP Central Committee decision "On Resolute Support for the Revolutionary Masses of the Left," announced 23 January 1967, implemented Mao's orders that "[t]he PLA should actively support the revolutionary leftists."[223] It called upon the PLA to lend "active support" to the Maoist faction and, if necessary, "send out troops to support them positively." Opponents were branded as counterrevolutionaries, who were to be "resolutely suppressed." If they resisted, "the army should strike back with force." Implementing instructions issued by the Military Commission of the Central Committee on 28 January purported to set guidelines for PLA "support the left" activities.[224] The PLA would take "resolute measures of dictatorship against conclusively proven" rightists and counterrevolutionaries. Within the PLA, however, the struggle would be tempered: "Handling of contradictions among the people in the same way as dealing with the enemy is not permitted." Arrest of PLA members without orders was forbidden, as was corporal punishment.

In this time of crisis, as was the case during the period when the PRC was established and consolidated, military control committees were created to exercise direct military administrative and legal control throughout China. The 11 February 1967 Proclamation announcing the establishment of the Peking Municipal Military Control Comittee stated that "criminal acts supported by iron-clad evidence shall be dealt with by the Military Control Committee according to law."[225] Within a fortnight the Peking military control committee announced the banning of certain factions and the arrest of their leaders.[226] On 16 February 1968 Vice-

45

Premier Hsieh Fu-chih introduced a five-man military control committee for the Supreme Court and announced: "The Center has decided to impose military control on all organs of dictatorship."[227] Similar supervisory "three-way alliances" of revolutionary cadres and the masses, led by PLA members, were also to be imposed on the Supreme People's Procuratorate and "practically all government organs and agencies." Military control over Kung-chien-fa was subsequently established throughout most of China. The PLA was authorized to dispatch "Central Support-the-Left Units" to "take up posts in every military region and provincial military district to carry out the task of supporting the left."[228] The PLA was granted authority to "pursue and arrest" opponents and "charge them and punish them according to law."[229]

Virtually all state institutions were placed under the direct control of the CCP. The 1973 Party Constitution proclaimed that state organs, the PLA and militia, labor unions and social organizations "must all accept the centralized leadership of the Party."[230] This situation of direct Party control was reflected in the new state constitution adopted by the Maoists in 1975. Calling the CCP "the core of leadership of the whole Chinese people," the new constitution declared that the PLA and militia were "led by the Communist Party of China" and that "the Chairman of the Central Committee of the Communist Party of China commands the country's armed forces."[231]

While the courts were not formally abolished during the Cultural Revolution, they functioned only sparingly. More often, serious cases were handled by mass trials, "revolutionary committees," or organs of the military control committees.[232]

Despite the exigencies of an obviously chaotic situation, some internal checks apparently were initially maintained within the legal system even though much of it had come under military control. Honan radio announced in May 1968 that death sentences pronounced by the Chengchou City Military Control Committee had been reviewed and approved by the Supreme People's Court.[233] Some subsequent cases, however, apparently were not reviewed. In March 1970 the Kunmin Municipality Military Control Committee in Kunmin Province announced a number of sentences, including fifteen death sentences, which "were executed immediately," evidently with no appeal or review allowed.[234]

The complete triumph of the societal model of justice during the Cultural Revolution period is demonstrated in three representative court decisions of various military control committees.[235] In a January 1971 decision of a county military control committee in Yunnan Province,[236] four local defendants were sentenced: an "American imperalist spy" and an "American and Chiang spy" were each sentenced to twenty years' imprisonment; one "counterrevolutionary" of "landlord family background" was sentenced to ten years, "in accordance with the party policy of 'dealing leniently with those who confess and severely with those who resist' "; and a "current counterrevolutionary" of "landlord family background" who, "although she was criticized and educated by the mases several times, she still refused to repent and reform herself," was sentenced "to be placed under control for five years."[237] The tribunal utilized the sentencing notice as an opportunity to educate the masses:

> We severely warn a handful of class enemies: you have already fallen into the vast expanses of the ocean of people's war. Your only way out is to turn yourselves in and confess your crime. If you put up a stubborn resistance, you will definitely be subjected to severe punishment by the iron fist of the dictatorship of the proletariat.[238]

Twenty-two criminals were sentenced by the military control committee of Szu-Mao region, Yunnan Province, on February 11, 1972.[239]

Among the offenses punished were killing, burglary, and "undermining a military marriage."[240] Three "bandit Chiang spies" and two killers were sentenced by the military control committee of Meng-lien county in Yunnan Province on 8 August 1972. Three received twenty-year prison terms, while two received "lenient" sentences of five and fifteen years based on their confessions.[241]

None of the three military control committee decisions cite any legal authority under which they operated, nor any laws or statutes applied to determine the various senences, other than the phrases "according to law" and "in accorance with party policy." Neither is any mention made of any defense of the accused. "Lenient treatment" was often given to those who confessed, and more severe treatment was threatened for "those who resist." These policies would discourage an accused from attempting a defense or challenging any evidence presented by the authorities.

The formal military legal system was not spared by the Maoists' attacks on Kung-chien-fa. The system of military courts and procuracies was "dismantled" during the Cultural Revolution, and would not be officially revived until October 1978.[242] The administration of military justice was left to party organs. All disciplinary actions (as well as important questions of any kind)[243] were required to be discussed in and approved by the unit Party committees before being carried out by the commanders or political commissars.[244] Mao's name and doctrines were widely incorporated into new editions of the military disciplinary and administrative regulations.[245] Mao's doctrine of the class nature of justice was embodied in Article 3 of the 1975 discipline regulations, in which leaders were admonished to apply Mao's doctrine of contradictions[246] to disciplinary cases:

48

> Strictly distinguish and correctly handle contradictions of two
> different natures and conscientiously grasp policies. As to
> mistakes in the nature of contradictions among the people,
> the guidelines of unite-criticize-unite, learn from past
> mistakes to avoid future ones, and cure the illness to save the
> patient should be resolutely upheld. As to contradictions
> between ourselves and the enemy or criminal elements who
> violate criminal law, disposition should be made according to
> law with reference to specifics of the case.

According to Mao's doctrine, even in the most serious cases (such as counterrevolution), offenders were to be more leniently treated if they were members of favored classes such as the army or other government offices. Capital punishment was not to be employed for these offenders "not because they have done nothing to deserve death, but because killing them would bring no advantage, whereas sparing their lives would."[247]

The PLA's supervision over Kung-chien-fa gradually receded until "normalcy" was again restored in 1973. The extensive involvement of the PLA in the Chinese administrative and legal structure during the Cultural Revolution might seem, on its face, to be a violation of Mao's oft-quoted dictum that "the Party commands the gun and the gun must never be allowed to command the Party."[248] Closer examination, however, reveals that this was not a putsch carried out by those espousing "the strictly military viewpoint," but rather a mobilization of a political army, under the firm control of Mao's party function, in furtherance of their political goals. Premier Chou En-lai sought to refute a civilian versus military analysis of the Cultural Revolution by explaining to American journalist Edgar Snow that "we are all connected with the army, and the army connects all of us."[249]

49

V.   MILITARY LAW IN POST-MAO CHINA

A.   Introduction

Since the death of Mao Tse-tung in September 1976 and the subsequent ouster of the "Gang of Four,"[250] China has entered a new era of reform and limited liberalization. One of the most notable developments has been the commitment of the more pragmatic post-Mao leadership led by Deng Xiaoping to a stable legal order and a regularized system of justice. The new leadership has recognized the need for strengthened legal institutions to guard against such arbitrary abuses as occurred during Mao's Cultural Revolution (the blame for which has subsequently been shifted to "renegades"):

> Having had enough of a decade of turmoil caused by Lin Biao and the Gang of Four, the people want law and order more than anything else. Democratization and legalization which the Chinese people have been yearning for are now gradually becoming a reality.[251]

In response to the lawlessness of the Cultural Revolution, China has made considerable progress in restoring the respectability of the jural model of law, in stressing rule by law over rule by man, and in providing a degree of regularization and normalization to its restored legal system.

In March 1978 a new state constitution was adopted which mitigated some of the more radical features of the 1975 version.[252] The new constitution revived the rights of the accused to defense and to an open trial.[253] The procuracy was also restored.[254]

In October 1978 Minister of Public Security Zhao Cangbi delivered a speech on strengthening the legal system in which he called for the enactment of a criminal code, a civil code, and numerous environmental and economic laws.[255] That minister Zhao was speaking with authority was evident from the December 1978 declaration of the CCP Central Committee:

> In order to safeguard people's democracy, it is imperative to strengthen the socialist legal system so that democracy is systemized and written into law in such a way as to insure the stability, continuity and full authority of this democratic system and these laws. There must be laws for people to follow, these laws must be observed, their enforcement must be strict and lawbreakers must be dealt with. From now on legislative work should have an important place on the agenda of the National People's Congress and its Standing Committee. Procuratorial and judicial organizations must maintain their independence as is appropriate; they must faithfully abide by the laws, rules and regulations, serve the people's interests, keep to the facts; guarantee the equality of all people before the people's laws and deny anyone the privilege of being above the law.[256]

The Party's call was answered by the Fifth National People's Congress. Numerous codes and laws were enacted beginning in 1979, to include the Criminal Law,[257] the Criminal Procedure Law,[258] and organic laws for the People's Courts[259] and the People's Procuratorates.[260] Under the new organic laws, the restored legal system reviewed many of the verdicts decided during the Cultural Revolution; between 1977 and mid-1980 more than 2,800,000 "unjust verdicts" were reversed.[261]

The renewed ascendancy of the jural model of law reached new heights with the enactment of China's latest Constitution in December 1982.[262] An attempt to institutionalize the rule of law is apparent in Article 5, which proclaims that "(a)ll state organs, the armed forces, all political parties and public organizations and all enterprises and undertakings must abide by the Constitution and the law." For the first time, legal restrictions are placed upon the Communist Party. The direct command of the PLA is removed from the CCPCC, at least formally, and vested in the newly established state Central Military Commission (Article 93).

The new Constitution proclaims that all citizens "are equal before the law" (Article 33). Unlike the 1954 version, the 1982 Constitution defines citizen as anyone "holding the nationality of" the PRC. Disfavored classes need no longer be excluded from citizenship because, according to the preamble, they "have been eliminated in our country." "However," it warns, "class struggle will continue to exist within certain limits for a long time to come." The new Constitution does not continue the 1978 Constitution's citizens duty to support the leadership of the CCP.[263] Nevertheless, CCP control is confirmed by the continued adherence to the "Four Basic Principles" delineated by Deng Xiaoping in March 1979 as the basis of China's new "socialist legality":[264] (1) the leadership of the CCP; (2) the guidance of Marxism-Leninism-Mao Tse-tung thought; (3) adherence to the people's democratic dictatorship (i.e. the dictatorship of the proletariat); and (4) following the socialist road.[265] Under the tutelage of these principles, China's socialist legal system continues to amount to the policy of the CCP transformed and solidified into legal form, although its operation is generally more reasonable and predictable than in the past.

The restoration of the formal military legal system began on 20 October 1978 with the announcement that, "in accordance with the PRC Constitution," the PLA military courts were officially revived.[266] The restoration was hailed as "an important organizational measure for strengthening our army's legal system and is of tremendous significance for grasping the key link in running the army well and fulfilling the general task for the new period." As part of the general national campaign for strengthening the legal system, the military polical and legal organs would be "reviving and perfecting legal procedures in order to effectively protect socialist democracy and the legitimate rights and intersts of cadres and

52

fighters throughout the army, and to deal blows to sabotage activities of class enemies and criminals." Lin Biao and the Gang of Four were assigned the blame for having "distintegrated" the military's Kung-chien-fa during the Cultural Revolution, which had "gravely undermined the legal system of our army"; now the new military legal system would, it was promised, reinvestigate cases decided during the Cultural Revolution in order to quickly reverse injustices."[267] The restoration of military judicial organs at local levels,[268] as well as representative military court cases,[269] were soon publicly announced.

The military procuracy officially resumed operations on 25 January 1979.[270] A conference of chief military procurators from various PLA units met from 26 February to 2 March 1979 for training and study of relevant procuratorial documents, to include the newly-issued state arrest and detention act.[271] Huan Yukun, deputy director of the PLA General Political Department, admonished the conferees to "become dauntless prosecutors who have no fear of dying in the course of their duties."[272]

One of the greatest difficulties to be overcome in the restoration of the legal system was a critical shortage of trained lawyers and legal workers. The president of the Supreme People's Court announced at the National Conference of Presidents of Higher People's Courts and Military Tribunals in July 1979 that all legal workers above the level of assistant judge would be required to complete a training course within three years.[273]

Besides those trained for military legal work, thousands of PLA personnel were subsequently trained and transferred to civilian legal positions. This enabled the rapidly-expanding system to be staffed with reliable personnel of "good ideology and working style."[274]

Two-month courses were soon commenced at national and local levels to train civilian and army political and judicial workers for the campaign to publicize the new legal system and its relation to "democracy and the four modernizations."[275] Political and legal cadres from local PLA units were trained in the importance of establishing the legal system and achieving its purposes: "base [your] work on the facts and the law, get rid of the idea of privilege, correct illegal activities such as issuing random orders, making random arrests and forcing confessions from people. . . ."[276] Similar campaigns within the PLA to study the legal system contine to this day. On 1 June 1986 the PLA instituted a new three-year program to educate soldiers on China's developing legal system, as part of a similar five-year nationwide campaign.[277] The political basis for the campaign is explained in the PLA General Political Department's implementing circular: "To earnestly popularize legal knowledge, consciously observe party discipline and state law, and safeguard and respect state laws under the new historical conditions is an important political task for the Army."[278]

B.   Structure

1.   Military Courts and Procuracies

The military courts of the PRC are authorized by the Constitution as an integral part of the state judicial system.[279] They are organized under the Organic Law of the People's Courts,[280] and assigned the common tasks of the people's court system:

> (T)o punish all offenders . . . so as to safeguard the system of the dictatorship of the proletariat, the socialist legal system, and social order, . . . citizens' prsonal, democratic rights and to guarantee the smooth progress of the socialist revolution and socialist construction.

54

The people's courts devote all their activities to educating citizens to be loyal to their socialist motherland and to voluntarily observe the Constitution and laws.[281]

The military procuracies are also authorized by the Constitution,[282] and organized under the Organic Law of the People's Procuratorates.[283] For the functional and organizational details of the military courts and procuratorates, the organic laws refer to separate enactments to be prescribed by the Standing Committee of the National People's Congress.[284] These laws are classified under China's broad state and military secrets regulations, and have not been published.[285] Nevertheless, considerable information concerning the organization and functions of the military justice organs can be found in available sources.

The Supreme People's Court is the highest organ in the military legal system. As of 1985, no separate military division had been established alongside the court's general divisions (two criminal, one civil, one economic). The task of reviewing military cases was assigned to sections within the criminal divisions.[286]

The Military Court of the People's Liberation Army is the highest military court below the Supreme Court, corresponding to the higher people's courts established for provinces, autonomous regions, and special municipalities. Tian Jia was named president of the court in 1982.[287] The Military Procuratorate of the PLA, under Chief Procurator Yu Kefa, is the highest military procuratorial organ below the Supreme People's Procuratorate.[288] Military courts and procuracies exist at the military region level, at the armed service level (army, navy, airforce), at the general department level (unified staff, political and logistical departments supporting all branches of the PLA), and in each large unit, reportedly down to regimental echelons.[289] The military judges are named by the Ministry of Defense,[290] and the military courts are directly responsible to the

Ministry of Defense, although they are also under the supervision of the Supreme People's Court.[291]   As an integral part of the state judicial system, the military courts employ the same procedural rules as the civilian courts.[292]

2.   Sources of Law

A considerable body of law has now been developed for application to the case of the PLA soldier who violates law or discipline. In major cases involving serious crimes or grave breaches of discipline, the soldier may undergo judicial punishment under the provisions of the Criminal Law, a supplementary military criminal law, or other state laws. For cases of lesser gravity, commanders, commissars, and party committees will collectively administer nonjudicial punishment under the PLA Discipline Regulations. These sources of law will be examined in turn.

a.   The Criminal Law

The main purpose of the Chinese criminal justice system is to protect, first of all, the socialist order, and next, the personal rights of citizens. The Criminal Law[293] fulfills this purpose by using "criminal punishments to struggle against all counterrevolutionary and other criminal conduct" in order to:

(1)   defend the system of the dictatorship of the proletariat,

(2)   protect socialist property of the whole people and property collectively owned by the laboring masses,

(3)   protect citizen's lawful privately-owned property,

(4)   protect citizen's rights of the person, democratic rights, and other rights,

(5)   maintain social order, order in production, order in work, order in education and research, and order in the lives of the masses of people, and

(6)   safeguard the smooth progress of the socialist revolution and the work of socialist construction.[294]

Crime is defined as any act which endangers the state, the socialist system, or society, and which is punishable by the Criminal Law. Eight categories of crimes and their specific penalties are listed in the Special Part. These offenses are:

(1)   crimes of counterrevolution,

(2)   crimes of endangering public security,

(3)   crimes of undermining the socialist order,

(4)   crimes of infringing upon the rights of the person and the democratic rights of citizens,

(5)   crimes of property violation,

(6)   crimes of disrupting the administrative order of society,

(7)   crimes of disrupting marriage and the family, and

(8)   dereliction of duty.[295]

The types of principal punishments applicable are:

(1)   Control (a type of supervised labor with the offender remaining in society), which may range from three months to two years;

(2)   Criminal detention (which may include compensation and one or two days leave per month), which may range from fifteen days to six months;

(3)   Fixed term imprisonment for six months to fifteen years (in prison or at "reform through labor" institutions for those physically able to labor);

(4)   Life imprisonment;

(5)   The death penalty (including the traditional death penalty with suspension of execution for two years), executed by shooting.

To these are added supplementary penalties of fines, deprivation of political rights, and confiscation of property.[296]

The Criminal Law does not apply retroactively, as did the 1951 counterrevolutionary statute. Acts committed before the implementation of the Criminal Law are governed by the laws, decrees and policies applicable at the time of the offense.[297]   While the presumption of innocence is still not adopted in Chinese law, provisions of the criminal procedure code afford some protections by requiring all evidence to be verified,[298] by prohibiting illegal means of gathering evidence such as torture, threat or enticement,[299] and by prohibiting convictions based solely on the defendant's confession.[300] The Criminal Law continues the

58

traditional practices of rewarding voluntary surrender,[301] and, with certain restrictions, the application of analogy.[302]

b.   The Military Criminal Law

Until 1982 the PLA had never operated under a unified criminal code governing military crimes.[303] Such a code was needed, according to the PLA General Political Department, in order to:

(1) strengthen the army legal system,

(2) correctly punish servicemen for their criminal offenses against their duties, *

(3) educate the large numbers of commanders and fighters in strictly abiding by the state's laws and honestly executing their duties, and

(4) consolidate and enhance the army's combat effectiveness.[304]

On 10 June 1981, the NPC Standing Committee adopted a military criminal law, the PRC Provisional Regulations on Punishing Servicemen Who Commit Offenses Against Their Duties,[305] which was implemented 1 January 1982. As part of the CCP campaign to strengthen the legal system, and in contrast with the usual treatment of military matters as state secrets, the law was announced and published in the press. The new military criminal law was adopted as "a supplement and continuation of the Criminal Law" to cover crimes committed by servicemen which are not written into the Criminal Law.[306] Crimes committed by servicemen which are not covered by the military criminal law "will be handled in accordance with the related articles of the Criminal Law."[307] Violations of military

59

discipline which are "not punishable by criminal penalty" are not covered by the law.[308]   Such disciplinary violations are subject to non-judicial punishment under the PLA Discipline Regulation.[309]   Minor violations of the military criminal law may also be "dealt with in accordance with military discipline" (Article 2).

The purpose of the military criminal law is "to wage struggle by means of penalty against all crimes against servicemen's duties and the state's military interests, to ensure victory in war and smooth progress in the army's modernization."[310]   Because servicemen's crimes may cause "much greater harm" to the state, the law imposes "severer punishment for servicemen than for civilians for similar crimes."[311]

The various military offenses and their minimum and maximum penalties established by the law are summarized in the table below.

Table 1

Table of Military Crimes and Punishments*

(Authorized by the Provisional Regulations

of the PRC on Punishing Servicemen Who Commit

Offenses Against Their Duties, adopted

6 June 1981, effective 1 January 1982)

GENERAL OFFENSES

ARTICLE		PEACETIME			WARTIME
		MAXIMUM CONFINEMENT	DEATH		
3	Illegal abuse of firearms and equipment	3 years	No		————
	- particularly serious cases	3-7 years	No		————
4(a)	Betraying or losing state military secrets	7 years	No		3 years to life
(b)	Stealing, collecting furnishing secrets to enemies	10 years to life	Yes		————
5	Leaving place of duty/ neglecting duty	7 years	No		5-7 years
6	Desertion (non-combat)	3 years	No		3-7 years

7	Illegally crossing the border (attempting to flee the PRC)	3 years	No	"more severe"
	- particularly serious cases	3-10 years	No	"more severe"
8	Permitting others to cross the border illegally	5 years	No	"more severe"
	- particularly serious cases	over 5 years	No	"more severe"
9	Maltreatment of subordinates - causing injury or grave consequences	5 years	No	————
	- causing death	over 5 years	No	————
10	Obstructing by force or threat the performance of duty of others	5 years	No	"more severe"
	- particularly serious cases	over 5 years	No	"more severe"
	- causing severe injury or death	Life	Yes	"more severe"
11	Theft of weapons or materiel	5 years	No	"more severe"
	- particularly serious cases	5 years to life	No	death
12	Sabotage	3 years	No	"more severe"
	- particularly serious cases	3 years to life	Yes	"more severe"

B. COMBAT OFFENSES

ARTICLE		MAXIMUM CONFINEMENT	DEATH
13	Self-inflicted injury to evade duty	3 years	No
	- particularly serious cases	3-7 years	No
14(a)	Spreading rumors harmful to morale	3 years	No
	- particularly serious cases	3-10 years	No
14(b)	Colluding with the enemy to spread rumors harmful to morale	10 years to life	No
	- particularly serious cases	————	Yes
15	Abandoning wounded on the battlefield	3 years	No
16	Desertion from the battlefield	3 years	No
	- particularly serious cases	3-10 years	No
	- causing major battle loses	10 years to life	Yes
17	Disobedience of orders in battle	3-10 years	No
	- causing serious harm to war effort	10 years to life	Yes
18	False reports/falsifying orders	3-10 years	No
	- causing serious harm to war effort	10 years to life	Yes

19(a)	Voluntary surrender	3-10 years	No
	- particularly serious cases	10 years to life	No
19(b)	Aiding the enemy as a prisoner	10 years to life	Yes
20	Plundering or harming innocent residents in operational areas	7 years	No
	- serious cases	over 7 years	No
	- particularly serious cases	life	Yes
21	Maltreatment of captives	3 years	No

* This table does not include common crimes, counterrevolutionary offenses, and other offenses against the state which are included in the PRC Criminal Law.

c.   The PLA Discipline Regulation

Nonjudicial punishment is administered in accordance with the provisions of the PLA Discipline Regulation promulgated in 1984.[312] The regulation reflects the accumulated experience and philosophy of the Chinest Communist military legal system. The role of military law in fulfilling two paramount policy goals is clearly outlined: first, that military law reinforces the political nature of the PLA and recognizes the leading role of the CCP; and second, that military law operates to maintain discipline and efficiency of operation through a system of formal and administrative legal procedures.

The regulation summarizes the basic purposes for military discipline in the PLA as follows:

1.   Implementing the line, principles and policies of the Communist Party of China, and obeying the state's Constitution, laws and regulations;

2.   Implementing the various orders, rules and regulations of the Army;

3.   Implementing orders, directives, and instructions of the higher level;

4.   Implementing the Three Main Rules of Discipline and the Eight Points for Attention.[313]

The regulation establishes both rewards and punishments to reward outstanding performance, maintain discipline, and educate the troops. Rewards of commendation, medals of merit (of three classes) and personal or unit honorary title are conferred for such actions as outstanding duty performance, rescue and relief, and for "inventions and creations."[314]

The purpose of punishment is to "learn from past mistakes to avoid future ones and to cure the illness to save the patient" by reforming the violator's behavior.[315] In accordance with these principles, the regulation provides for a graduated system of disciplinary punishments to be administered at various command levels, depending on the grade of the offender and the gravity of the offense:

1.   Warning;

2.   Serious warning;

3.   Demerit;

4.   Major demerit;

5.   Demotion from position (rank);

6.   Dismissal from office;

7.   Dismissal from military status.[316]

The enumerated disciplinary violations for which these punishments are applied are:

1.   Violating the policy of the Party and the Constitution, laws and regulations of the state;

2. Violating and disobeying orders, violating codes, regulations, institutions and systems;

3. Displaying a negative attitude in combat, cowardice in combat, failure to grasp combat opportunities;

4. Acting individually without orders or coordination from superiors and thereby hindering coordinated operations;

5. Damaging or losing public property, weapons, or equipment, or causing incidents due to violations of institutions;

6. Revelation of state and military secrets;

7. Failure to perform duties, delaying work;

8. Absence without leave, or failure to return from leave on time;

9. Threatening superiors or others with weapons;

10. Fighting, or disturbing the public order;

11. Obscene or indecent conduct, dissolute behavior;

12. Theft of public or private property;

13. Gambling, smuggling, speculation;

14. Seeing a danger and not assisting;

15. Counterblows and vengeance, framing others, making false accusations, or creating rumors;

16. Unprincipled behavior, condoning wrongdoers and violations;

17. Suppressing democracy and physically punishing subordinates;

18. Making falsities and fakes, and deceiving superiors;

19. Violating discipline in other aspects.[317]

    d.   Other Regulations

Under the PLA Discipline Regulation, violation of other state and military laws and regulations may be punished as a disciplinary offense.[318] Two of these regulations with frequent application are the PLA Internal Administration Regulation and the PLA Regulation on Safeguarding State and Military Secrets.

The Internal Administration Regulation[319] contains the general guidelines for the operation of the PLA. It outlines the duties and responsibilities of soldiers and company-level commanders, regulates military courtesies and uniform, and governs the daily management of soldiers, equipment and materiel.

The PLA Regulation on Safeguarding State and Military Secrets illustrates the acute sensitivity in China toward keeping "secrets," and implements the numerous state provisions for guarding secrets. The Constitution proclaims the citizen's duty to "keep state secrets" (Article 53). In 1951 the PRC promulgated the "Provisional Regulations for the Preservation of State Secrets," the continuing validity of which was affirmed in 1980.[320] The PLA issued its own implementing regulations on state and military secrets in 1956,[321] and again in 1978.[322] The PLA regulations contain broad "rules for the safekeeping of secrets":

1. Never discuss military secrets you shouldn't discuss.

2. Never ask questions about secrets you shouldn't know.

3. Never read secret documents you shouldn't read.

4. Never mention a secret in personal correspondence.

5. Never record secret information on anything other than secret information files.

6. Never discuss military secrets in places where such secrets should not be discussed.

7. Never take secret documents to public places or to the homes of relatives or friends.

8. Never discuss party, state or military secrets in front of family members, including your own children.

9. Never use public telephones, clear language telegrams or civilian post offices for handling secret information.[323]

Violations of state and military secrets regulations are punishable as disciplinary violations,[324] as military crimes,[325] or under the Criminal Law.[326]

C. Process

The administration of military justice within PLA units is a joint responsibility of the Commander and the Political Officer.[327] Both are responsible for the overall operation of the unit, under the supervision of higher level "leaders" (commanders and political commissars) and the unit Party committees.[328] Under the Military Discipline Regulation, both the commander and the political officer have authority to administer disciplinary punishment. All disciplinary actions must be submitted to the unit's Party committee or branch for discussion and decision before being carried out by the leadership.[329]

1.   Nonjudicial Punishment

The PLA commander or political officer confronted with a violation of military discipline must first decide whether the offending soldier should, under the circumstances, be given disciplinary punishment or the less severe informal punishment of "education and criticism."[330] This informal penalty may be carried out privately or in the presence of the offender's fellow soldiers at a company-level criticism meeting, presided over by the deputy commander or political officer. The offender is expected to confess his wrong, make an oral or written self-criticism, and promise to reform.[331] "Struggle," a harsher informal penalty widely used during the Cultural Revolution, entails denunciation, intimidation, and at times violence, before a large audience.[332] New provisions in the 1984 Discipline Regulation appear to be directed toward prohibition of "struggle" in the PLA; direct and indirect physical punishment, scolding, and insulting personal diginity are now prohibited.[333]

If the violation is deemed serious enough, disciplinary punishment may be imposed after investigation and evaluation. The facts and circumstances of the offense, as well as its effect upon the unit, must be considered. The violator's own statement, his past record and degree of recognition of the offense, and "the opinions of the masses" must also be taken into account.[334] The investigation is to be handled in a timely manner, and punishment should be administered within two months.[335] Approval for extension of this time limit is required from higher authorities. The accused has a right to defense, but he is cautioned against trying to hinder the proceedings.[336] Should punishment be deemed appropriate, only one of the enumerated disciplinary punishments may be imposed.[337] Punishments may be announced face-to-face, before the troops, in meetings, or in writing, "in order to educate the violator and the troops."[338] If the violator does not accept his punishment, he may petition for appeal within ten days; however, execution of the punishment is not suspended during the petition period.[339] Superiors are required to act on the appeal in a timely manner, generally within two months.[340] If the appeal is held valid, the original punishment "should be corrected."[341]

Soldiers, as well as leaders, are entitled to bring accusations of disciplinary violations.[342] Accusations may be submitted through channels, or bypassing channels. False accusations constitute separate violations of the Discipline Regulation.[343]

The disciplinary penalties do not include confinement. However, temporary custody of up to seven days may be imposed upon soldiers who manifest signs of potential desertion, flight to avoid punishment, violence, or suicide.[344]

The actual operation of nonjudicial punishment in the PLA disciplinary system, and the dominant role played by Party organs, is illustrated in some reported representative cases:

71

(1)   Beginning in December 1980, leaders of an engineer and construction regiment in the Wuhan Military Region were misappropriating state funds.   The Party committee of the region's logistics department conducted an investigation and brought the situation to the attention of the regiment's Party committee.   The regimental Party committee administered disciplinary punishments of serious warning to both the regiment commander and to the regimental political commissar, which was reported in August 1981.[345]

(2)   In December 1983, some leading cadres of a division in the Beijing Military Region bribed proctors and allowed cheating in admissions examinations.   The offenses were investigated by the Military Region Party Committee, which administered disciplinary punishment.   The division commander and political commissar both received serious warnings, and the deputy political commissar, who was directly responsible, was dismissed from his position.   The chief examiner and proctor who accepted the bribes received criticism-education and "disciplinary measures."   Fifty-two students involved in the fraud had their names removed from enrollment lists.   The Military Region Party Committee issued a notice concerning the case for subordinate units to use "as a mirror" to rectify "unhealthy tendencies of using the power of office for private purposes and fraud." The notice was publicized in March 1984.[346]

2.   Judicial Punishment

Serious violations of the military criminal law may be punished by the military courts.   Cases involving minor violations of the military criminal law, "when not too much harm has been caused," might not be considered criminal offenses, but instead be dealt with "in accordance with military discipline."[347]

72

The functional responsibilities of the various components of the Chinese judicial system are outlined in the Criminal Procedure Law:

> The public security organs are responsible for investigation, detention, and preparatory examination in criminal cases. The people's procuracies are responsible for approving arrest, conducting procuratorial control (including investigation) and initiating public prosecution. The people's courts are responsible for adjudication. No other organ, organization or individual has the right to exercise these powers.[348]

The pretrial proceedings entail (1) detention and arrest, and (2) investigation. Arrest must be reported to the procuracy within three days (seven days in special circumstances), for approval within another three days.[349] If the arrest is approved, the suspect may be held pending investigation for up to two months (three months if approved by the procuracy of the next higher level).[350] Extortion of confessions by torture, and gathering of evidence by threat, enticement or deceit is forbidden.[351] After the investigation is complete, the procuracy decides whether to initiate a public prosecution before the courts. Prosecution is initiated by filing an indictment with a court.[352]

The jurisdiction of the military courts extends beyond active duty service members to include staff members and workers within the military establishment.[353] Chinese jurists have argued that this provision covers offenders who are civilian employees in military technical and academic capacities, since their familiarity and close connection with the military would involve the national military interest.[354] It is further argued that civilian joint offenders with military personnel should be punished under the stricter provisions of the military criminal law for offenses covered by that law.[355]

The Constitutional right to defense (Article 125), as implemented in the Criminal Procedure Law (Article 26), includes the right to a defense lawyer. However, that right apparently does not attach until "after the court has decided to open the court session and adjudciate the case," thus precluding pre-trial assistance.[356] The following functions for defense lawyers were specified in the 1980-81 trial of the Gang of Four:

(1) to protect the legitimate rights and interests of the defendants,

(2) to contribute to the correct handling of the trial in the Special Court,

(3) to publicize socialist democracy and socialist legality, and

(4) to help persuade the defendants to acknowledge guilt, obey the law, and accept reform.[357]

The primary-level military court is a collegial panel composed of one judge and two "people's assessors." Trials of first instance in higher-level courts may be heard by a panel of from one to three judges and from two to four assessors.[358] The military judge is a serving officer who has undergone juridical training, and is appointed by the Ministry of Defense.[359] The assessors are lay judges who are to represent the military masses and to participate in the conduct and decision of the trial. They are selected from prepared lists, and are also to have received some legal training.[360]

The Criminal Procedure Law provides for three stages in the trial process: (1) examination of evidence, (2) deliberation, and (3) judgment.[361] While trials in China are generally open to the public (unless "state secrets or the private affairs of individuals" are involved), military trials are open only to a military public.[362] After the opening formalities, the trial begins with questioning of the accused by the court members or, at their request, by the military procurator. After the panel has concluded its questioning, the victim and the defense may be allowed to put questions to the accused. Witnesses and material evidence are also examined. After the tribunal completes its inquiry, the military procurator and the victim may address the panel. Then the accused may make a statement, following which the defense attorney may conduct the defense. The court may allow debate, at the close of which the accused may make his final statement. The court then recesses to deliberate and render judgment, "based on the facts and evidence that have been clarified and based on the relevant laws."[363] The decision as to guilt or innocence, what crime was committed, and what punishment is to be applied, is announced publicly and posted in military areas.[364] Once a case reaches trial, having been investigated by both the security organs and the procuracy, conviction is virtually a certainty.[365]

Either the accused or the military procurator may appeal the decision of the court of first instance to the next higher level court, which must review the case and uphold, revise, or overturn the judgment.[366] Punishment may not be increased in cases appealed by defendants, but may be increased in cases appealed by the procurator. The decision of the reviewing court is final. Death sentences are to be reviewed by the Supreme People's Court, whether appealed or not.[367] Sentences to imprisonment are served in military prisons.[368]

Under the Criminal Procedure Law, criminal complaints and accusations may be filed by citizens with the public security organs, the procuracy, or the courts.[369] The procedures for servicemen to follow in bringing criminal complaints directly to the attention of military courts were outlined by the editors of Zhongguo Fazhi Bao (China Legal Journal) on 2 May 1986, in response to a letter from a PLA recruit in Henan province.[370] Private prosecutions may be commenced before military courts under the provisions of the Criminal Procedure Law, with the additional requirement that the unit Party committee assist in the investigation and production of evidence. If supported by sufficient evidence, the case may be transferred to the military procuracy for initiation of public prosecution, or may be directly investigated and heard by the military court as a private prosecution. If the evidence is insufficient to support a criminal prosecution, the case may be referred to the complainant's unit Party committee for further investigation. If sufficient evidence is developed, the unit Party committee may refer the case back to the court. Violations that do not constitute criminal offenses may be referred for possible disciplinary action. The law requires that complainants be informed of the potential legal responsibility incurred for false accusations.[371]

The actual operation of the Military legal system in post-Mao China is difficult to assess. The examination and analysis of the textual provisions of statutes and regulations, and drawing conclusions as to their meaning and importance, may produce a distorted image of their application in actual practice. Reports of actual cases and the procedures employed therein would be helpful, but are, unfortunately, rare. Those few that are publicized are generally done so for political purposes, to illustrate a new mass campaign or to deliver a warning. Nevertheless, they do illustrate the growing role of the military court system in maintaining stability and discipline within the PLA while responding to political and legal developments.

A case tried before the Military Court of the Logistics Department of Chengtu Military Region was publicized in Jiefangjun Bao (Liberation Army Daily) to coincide with the restoration of the military court system in December 1978.[372] A supply depot deputy chief of staff and two subordinates were accused of taking bribes, embezzlement and theft. As the military procuracy had not yet been restored, the case was investigated by a special Party study group. After considerable material evidence and the testimony of witnesses was presented, the accused all admitted their guilt. The military court sentenced the three accused to prison terms ranging from six to ten years, and expelled them from both the Party and the army.

D.   Law of War

China has long had its own customs and traditions concerning the conduct of warfare, derived from its vast historical experience. Western principles of international humanitarian law developed comparatively recently, and these began to be assimilated in China only in the latter part of the nineteenth century. Since that time, China has been active in the formation of the multilateral agreements establishing the international laws of armed conflict.

Following her participation in the Hague Conferences of 1899 and 1907, China ratified eleven of the Hague Conventions.[373] The Republic of China later ratified the 1925 Geneva Protocol prohibiting the use in war of asphyxiating and poisonous gases,[374] and the 1929 Geneva Conventions on prisoners of war, the wounded and sick.[375] The ROC participated in the 1949 Geneva Diplomatic Conference that concluded the four Geneva Conventions now in general force but, although it signed these conventions, it never ratified them.[376]

In 1947, during the civil war which ended with the establishment of the PRC, the CCP announced that it would not be bound by "any treaties which disgrace the country and strip away its rights" conceded by the

77

Nationalist government after 10 January 1946.[377]   This policy was modified somewaht in the PRC's first outline constitution, the Common Program, which proclaimed that the Communist government would examine all treaties and agreements concluded by the Nationalist government, and would "recognize, abrogate, revise or re-negotiate them according to their respective contents."[378]   In accordance with this policy, the PRC announced on 13 July 1952 that it would "recognize" the Nationalist government's accession to the 1925 Geneva gas protocol, and its signature to the 1949 Geneva Conventions.[379] The PRC's formal ratification of the Geneva Conventions was deposited on 28 December 1956.[380]

In recent years, the PRC has become more active in the development of the international laws of armed conflict. In 1981 the PRC ratified the United Nations Conventional Weapons Convention.[381]   A PRC delegation participated in the first session (1974) of the Geneva Diplomatic Conference on Humanitarian Law (1974-77) which drafted two protocols additional to the 1949 Geneva Conventions,[382] and the PRC became the first permanent member of the UN security counsel to ratify both protocols on 14 September 1983.[383]

1.   Protection of Prisoners of War

Humanitarian principles governing the treatment of prisoners of war (P.O.W.s) were recognized in China as early as the fourth century B.C., when Sun Tzu wrote: "Treat the captives well, and care for them."[384] The Sung dynasty code of 963 A.D. prescribed death by beheading for a soldier who killed an enemy who had given up his arms during armed conflict or who had deserted and had come to surrender.[385]

Mao Tse-tung, a careful student of Sun Tzu, strongly advocated a pragmatic approach to the treatment of P.O.W.s.   He considered humanitarian treatment of P.O.W.s to be a powerful propaganda tool and a potential source of strength to his nascent Red Army. In 1929 he wrote, "Preferential treatment of captives is an effective method of propagandizing to the enemy forces."[386] Mao prescribed a five-part plan to both propagandize the enemy and strengthen his own forces by using captives: (1) "refrain from searching them for money and things"; (2) welcome captives warmly and do not insult them; (3) give captives equal material treatment as the Red Army soliders; (4) propagandize captives, and allow those who do not wish to remain to leave; and (5) give the captives medical attention and monetary allowances equal to those received by the Red Army.[387] When returned captives spread their stories of good Red Army treatment among their fellow, often ill-treated conscripts, they would be more likely to defect and less likely to fight effectively. This policy of preferential treatment of captives was taught in the basic training of new recruits and incorporated as the eighth point of attention in the Red Army disciplinary rules: "Do not ill-treat captives."[388]

After the intervention of the PLA in the Korean Conflict in 1950, humanitarian treatment of P.O.W.s did not suit the dictates of communist policy. United Nations troops taken prisoner by the PLA found that their treatment depended on the extent to which they were willing to cooperate under the Chinese "lenient policy." This ill-named policy was based on the communist allegation that the Korean war was one of American aggression and part of a capitalist conspiracy against peace:

> The Chinese claimed that all United Nations prisoners taking part in this unjust war were war criminals, and that if they were captured their captors had the right to kill them. But, the Chinese argument went on, the soldiers of the "aggressors" were, after all, ordinary working men who had been duped and misled by their reactionary rulers. Therefore prisoners would not be summarily executed (hence the

"leniency") but would be given the opportunity to reach a state of remorse and repentance for their crimes.[389]

Having defined the Korean conflict as a capitalist war of aggression, the PRC held that the UN troops were "war criminals" deserving punishment, not protection. Under the "lenient policy," P.O.W.'s were subjected to harsh conditions and brutal treatment as they underwent "re-education."[390] Over 5,000 American prisoners of war died because of Chinese and North Korean "war atrocities," and more than a thousand survivors were victims of war crimes.[391]

On its side, the PRC accused the UN of illegal treatment and "barbarous massacres" of Chinese prisoners of war.[392] But at the end of the war, seventy-one percent of the Chinese P.O.W.s held by the UN Command refused repatriation to the PRC, electing instead to join the Nationalists on Taiwan.[393]

Since the Korean War, and since formally ratifying the Geneva Conventions, the PRC's treatment of prisoners of war has gradually improved. During the 1962 border conflict with India, the PRC captured over 3,900 prisoners of war. India protested the faiure to the PRC to grant access to the prisoners by the International Committee of the Red Cross (ICRC), or the Indian Red Cross Society. Further protests were lodged against the parading of 27 Indian officers in various Chinese cities, and against PRC attempts to indoctrinate Indian prisoners of war.[394] Nevertheless, there were no allegations of the types of atrocities committed during the Korean conflict.

During China's 1979 border conflict with Vietnam, both parties accepted the services of the International Committee of the Red Cross, and allowed it access to prisoners of war.[395] By 22 June 1979 a repatriation agreement concluded by the national Red Cross societies of the two countries had been carried out, with 1,636 Vietnamese and 238 Chinese P.O.W.s repatriated.[396] The Vietnamese had been treated well by their Chinese captors.[397]

2. Suppression of Grave Breaches of the Law of War

The Geneva Conventions obligate each contracting party to "enact any legislation necessary to provide effective penal sanctions for persons committing, or ordering to be committed, any of the grave breaches" of the Conventions.[398] Grave breaches are defined as those involving any of the following acts, if committed against prisoners of war, civilians, the wounded, sick or shipwrecked, or others protected under the Conventions:

(1) willful killing,

(2) torture or inhuman treatment,

(3) compelling a protected person to serve in the forces of a hostile power,

(4) willfully depriving a protected person of rights of fair and regular trial prescribed in the Conventions,

(5) unlawful deportation, transfer or confinement of protected civilians, and

(6) extensive destruction and appropriation of property, not justified by military necessity and carried out unlawfully and wantonly.[399]

From the early civil war years, the Chinese Red Army included prohibitions against looting civilians, damaging civilian property and crops, and ill-treating captives in its disciplinary code, the Three Rules of Discipline and Eight Points for Attention.[400]   Although based on pragmatic and propaganda considerations, and only selectively enforced (those branded class enemies, counterrevolutionaries or war criminals were not protected), they served as a basis for further legal development. The military criminal law enacted in 1981 includes two articles which may be seen as providing at least some of the legal sanctions against war crimes mandated by the Geneva Conventions. Article 20 punishes soldiers who plunder and harm "innocent residents in military operational areas" with prison sentences (up to life imprisonment) or death. Serious maltreatment of captives may be punished with up to three years' imprisonment. Presumably soldiers who injure or kill prisoners of war may also be punished under the relevant articles of the Criminal Law.

The Geneva Conventions impose a further obligation to search out and try those who have committed grave breaches of the laws of war.[401] However, if the accused are prisoners of war, the failure to accord them rights of fair and regular trial would itself constitute a grave breach.[402]

After the Second World War, the Nationalist government tried 605 war crimes cases involving 883 Japanese defendants,[403] under the provisions of the 1946 Law Governing the Trial of War Criminals.[404] Before being forced from the mainland to Taiwan, the Nationalists terminated their program of war crimes trials and transferred many of the convicted Japanese war criminals to Tokyo to serve out their terms in the hands of the allied occupation authorities.[405] After the establishment of the PRC on the mainland, many Japanese accused of war crimes were held without trial until 1956. In June of that year the PRC, courting Japanese diplomatic recognition, announced a new "lenient policy": those Japanese who had "committed minor crimes or who had repented comparatively well" were to be dealt with leniently and not prosecuted; those who committed serious crimes should receive "lenient sentences according to their crimes and conduct while in custody"; those who had committed "crimes both during the war and further crimes on Chinese territory after the Japanese surrender should be dealt with according to the combined crimes."[406]

Special military courts were organized by the Supreme People's Court to try the remaining Japanese war criminals.[407] The accused were allowed to present a defense, and be represented by defense lawyers. In one such trial, eight defendants faced charges including mass slaughter of 1,280 villagers, killing of civilians and prisoners of war, and use of poison gas and "germ warfare."[408] The defendants all confessed and expressed their contrition before the court. The military court adjudged prison sentences ranging from twelve to twenty years, with the time already spent in custody deducted from the terms. Two days after this trial, the Supreme People's Procuratorate released 335 Japanese accused of war crimes, because they "had shown repentance during their custody or . . . were lesser criminals."[409]

While the trial procedures received by the Japanese defendants were doubtlessly of at least equal fairness and regularity with any accorded PRC citizens at the time, it is questionable whether they can be considered as having met the minimum standards prescribed in the Conventions.[410]

The recent extensive development of the Chinese legal system includes provisions for a considerable number of procedural and substantive guarantees, to include right of defense and prohibition of any coercion of confessions. A strict application of these new legal standards in any future trials of war crimes suspects by military courts would go far toward fulfillment of the obligations imposed by the Geneva Conventions.

VI. CONCLUSIONS

The military legal system of Communist China has successfully performed a number of important functions since the PLA was first organized in 1927. It has, first of all, fulfilled the basic task of maintaining discipline which is common to all armed forces; only trained, disciplined armies, and not mobs, can win wars. At the same time, the military legal system has played an essential part in fulfilling the political aspects of miltiary discipline in the PLA. As we have seen, the maintenance of discipline in the Red Army was essential in securing the good will and support of the peasants during the civil wars. Mao taught that "Red Army discipline is a practical propaganda to the masses."[411] Undisciplined troops could have turned the peasants to active hostility, and Mao's guerilla "fish" would then have had no "water" to surround and protect them.[412] Instead, the military legal system was a means of achieving the politically-based discipline Mao outlined to govern relationships between officers and soldiers of the army, between the army and the people, and between captors and captives.[413] This "iron discipline" was sufficiently durable to weather years of civil war and resistance to Japan and to ultimately achieve the complete seizure of state power so long sought by the CCP. With power won, the CCP's army assumed an additional role as a national defense force, but the political aspect of discipline remained paramount. The first rule of discipline for the PLA, even before the traditional three main rules and eight points, remains "implementing the line, principles, and policies of the Communist Party of China."[414]

The military legal system has fulfilled a second function, as an important part of the development of the Chinese legal system as a whole. As we have seen, the military court system was the first formalized court system of Communist China, and the first to establish the roles of the procuracy and the assessors. Throughout the history of Communist China, the military legal system has been called upon in times of crisis to function as the main, and at times the sole, instrument for carrying out the judicial function. In civil war, at the beginning of the PRC, and during the Cultural Revolution, the military legal system was required to extend its scope and maintain order for much of Chinese society. In the post-Mao restoration and rapid expansion of "socialist legality," the military legal system has played a leading role and has proved to be a source for thousands of cadres to supply much of the national legal system with trained and politically reliable legal workers.

The Chinese legal heritage is reflected in the operation of the military legal system. The traditional preference for informal adjudication of disputes is apparent as the commanders and Party committees continue to handle cases of significant gravity through disciplinary rather than criminal procedures whenever practicable.[415] Several other traditional principles are maintained in the modern military legal system, to include sentencing by analogy, rewarding of voluntary surrender and confession, suspending execution of the death penalty for two years, and lack of a presumption of innocence. At the same time, considerable recent substantive and procedural development is evident. A formal, regularized system is now in place which provides significant procedural guarantees and safeguards. Even if their actual application is as yet unclear, the provisions for defense, strict requirements for collection and evaluation of evidence, and appellate rights provide a basis for optimism that a normalized system capable of giving the PLA offender reasonably fair treatment is emerging. The past class-oriented approach to justice is giving way before loud calls for "equality before the law."[416] The development of a legal system according equal treatment to the high and mighty as well as to the masses is viewed as essential in order to prevent disorders like those which wracked China during the Cultural Revolution, and as a prerequisite to economic development. This more egalitarian approach is reflected in the 1984 PLA Discipline Regulation, which no longer utilizes Mao's distinction between "contradictions among the people" as opposed to "contradictions between the enemy and ourselves"[417] as a basis for administering discipline, and in which directives to purge "class enemies" from the ranks of the PLA[418] no longer appear.

The modern Chinese military legal system still faces problems in its development. Internal PLA discipline problems are apparently at a serious enough level that a new supplement to the Three Main Rules of Discipline and the Eight Points for Attention is being introduced. The "Eight Prohibitions" are "new rules" for general enforcement:

(1)   prohibition against beating, swearing at, and corporal punishment for soldiers;

(2)   prohibition against receiving gifts from soldiers;

(3)   prohibition against infringement of soldiers' interets by cadres;

(4)   prohibition against imposing fines on soldiers;

(5)   prohibition against alcoholism;

(6)   prohibition against gambling;

(7)   prohibition against reading pornographic materials; and

(8)   prohibition against deception.[419]

Another problem for the Chinese military legal system is the lack of genuine independence. Statutes promising judicial independence do not mean that any real independence from the CCP exists. Like all Chinese institutions, courts must accept Party leadership. Nevertheless, the CCP has proclaimed its intention to allow courts to decide individual cases without undue outside influence: "[CCP] leadership refers mainly to leadership by means of policy and principle and political and ideological leadership, rather than interference in the judicial organs' exercise of their powers or replacing the judicial organs in the exericse of those powers."[420] Nevertheless, so long as Premier Deng's "Four Principles" (CCP leadership, Marxism-Leninism-Mao Tse-tung thought, people's democratic dictatorship, and socialist road) remain the basis for the operation of the military legal system, meaningful judicial independence cannot be achieved.

Despite continuing problems, expectations for sustained development of the Chinese military legal system arise from the fact that the attainment of "socialist legality" remains an important policy goal of the CCP. While it is most unlikely that the CCP will loosen its power over its state and its armed forces by establishing a truly independent legal system, CCP power need not be threatened by according PLA soldiers basically fair and equal treatment under the military legal system. The recent development of the military legal system indicates that a new criteria of basic procedural fairness is indeed being applied to its traditional functions: maintaining discipline and combat effectiveness in the world's largest armed forces; and maintaining the political unity of the army with the Chinese Communist Party.

ENDNOTES

1. The armed forces of the PRC are collectively entitled the Chinese People's Liberation Army (PLA). In 1986 the PLA had a total strength of approximately 2,950,000 (71.5% army, 11.9% navy, and 16.6% air force). 1987 Britannica Book of the Year 623.

2. Only one survey of the subject has appeared in the West. See Tsien, L'Evolution Actuelle de la Justice Militaire en Chine, 8 Recueils de la Societe Internationale de la Droit Penal Militaire et de Droit de la Guerre 177-86 (1981).

3. The term Communist China is used because the CCP's armed forces and military legal system pre-date the establishment of the PRC by over 20 years.

4. Military law has both a broad and a narrow sense. It has been defined as: "A system of regulations for the government of armed forces. That branch of the laws which respects military discipline and the government of persons employed in the military service." Black's Law Dictionary 896 (5th ed. 1979). "In its wider sense, it includes also that law which, operative only in time of war or like emergency, regulates the relations of enemies and authorizes military government and martial law." W. Winthrop, Military Law and Precedents 5 (2d ed. reprint 1920).

5. Chairman of the Chinese Communist Party from 1935 until his death in 1976. The pinyin system for transliterating Chinese, adopted by the PRC in 1979, is used herein for PRC names of persons and places

88

since that date. For names of persons and places before 1979, the more familiar Wade-Giles system of transliteration is retained.

6. Mao, <u>On Correcting Mistaken Ideas in the Party</u>, in Selected Military Writings of Mao Tse-tung 53, 54 (1968) [hereinafter Selected Military Writings].

7. <u>Ci Hai</u> 850 (1979) <u>quoted in</u> R. Dolan, <u>A Comparative English-Chinese Dictionary of Military Terms</u> 73 (U.S. Defense Intelligence Agency 1981).

8. Victor Li, <u>The Evolution and Development of the Chinese Legal System</u>, in China: Management of a Revolutionary Society 221 (J. Lindbeck ed. 1971).

9. Jerome Cohen, <u>The Criminal Process in the People's Republic of China, 1949-1963</u>, at 20 (1968).

10. Lubman, <u>Form and Function in the Chinese Criminal Process</u>, 69 Colum. L. Rev. 535, 566 (1969).

11. Leng, <u>The Role of Law in the People's Republic of China As Reflecting Mao Tse-tung's Influence</u>, 68 J. Crim. L. & Criminology 356 (1977).

12. For a comprehensive treatment of law in traditional China, see D. Bodde & C. Morris, <u>Law in Imperial China</u> (1967); Chu Tung-tsu, <u>Law and Society in Traditional China</u> (1961); and S. van der Sprenkel, <u>Legal Institutions in Manchu China</u> (1962).

13. <u>Ta Hsueh</u> (The Great Learning), in Masters of Chinese Political Thought 201, 202 (S. de Grazia ed. 1973).

14. <u>The Analects</u> VI:3.

15. For an exposition of the meanings and functions of <u>li</u> and <u>fa</u>, see Benjamin Schwartz, <u>On Attitudes Toward Law in China</u>, in Government Under Law and the Individual (M. Katz ed. 1957), <u>reprinted in</u> Jerome Cohen, <u>supra</u> note 9.

16. Bodde & Morris, <u>supra</u> note 12, at 23.

17. S. van der Sprenkel, <u>supra</u> note 12, at 29.

18. <u>See generally</u> Gelatt, <u>The People's Republic of China and The Presumption of Innocence</u>, 73 J. Crim. L. & Criminology 259 (1982), and Thieme, <u>The Debate on the Presumption of Innocence in the People's Republic of China</u>, 10 Rev. Socialist L. 277 (1984).

19. Bodde & Morris, <u>supra</u> note 12, at 33.

20. <u>See generally</u> Rickett, <u>Voluntary Surrender and Confession in Chinese Law: The Problem of Continuity</u>, 30 J. of Asian Stud. 797 (1971).

21. S. van der Sprenkle, <u>supra</u> note 12, at 68.

22. Bodde & Morris, <u>supra</u> note 12, ch. VI, sec. 3.

23. S. van der Sprenkle, <u>supra</u> note 12, at 69.

24. W. Scarborough, A Collection of Chinese Proverbs 88, 334 (C. Allen rev. 1926), in S. van der Sprenkle, supra note 12, app. 3.

25. Id. chs. 7-9.

26. S. B. Griffith, The Chinese People's Liberation Army 204 (1967).

27. Id. In an effort to overcome this negative attitude, the fledgling Chinese Workers' and Peasants' Red Army styled its troops "fighters" or "warriors" (chan-shih) rather than the odious "soldiers" (ping). Edgar Snow, Red Star Over China 280 (2d ed. 1944).

28. Griffith, supra note 26, at 210. The British strategist, Capt. B. H. Liddell Hart characterized Sun Tzu's classic as "the concentrated essence of wisdom on the conduct of war," even less dated than Clausewitz, despite being over 2,000 years older. Sun Tzu, The Art of War at v (S. Griffith trans. 1963).

29. Lee Ping-chai, The Military Legal System of the Republic of China, 14 Mil. L. Rev. 160 (1961).

30. Sun Tzu, supra note 28, at 127, 122.

31. Ch'ing Dynasty penal code. Translated in Ta Tsing Leu Lee (G. Staunton trans. 1810). The fifth division is composed of five books, totaling 70 sections.

32. Id. § 202.

33. Id. § 212.

34. Id. § 217.

35. Id. § 209. A second offense could merit 100 blows.

36. Id. § 210. A death sentence here could only be executed after two years' imprisonment; often the offender was pardoned or had his sentence reduced during this period. Other, more serious crimes, called for immediate execution.

37. Tsien, supra note 2, at 179.

38. Three representative trials of military defendants in the civilian court system are reported in Bodde & Morris, supra note 12, and summarized as follows:

> (1)   The Department for Kuangtung of the Board of Punishments sentenced Naval First Captain Ch'en P'an-kuei in 1807 to 60 blows with the heavy bamboo and one year penal servitude for diverting funds from his sailors' payroll to repair his ship's sails and other equipment, in violation of the Ch'ing code's prohibitions on exceeding authorizations for expenditures. Since none of the funds had been appropriated to his personal use, and because he had restored them, the Board recommended to the Board of War that Ch'en be reinstated to his Office, and that his punishment be remitted. Id. 478-80.

> (2)   In 1825, Sergeant Li Ch'ung-shen unlawfully attempted to mediate a debt dispute in Chihli province. In an attempt to force a confession, Sergeant

Li ordered his soldiers to beat one of the parties, Kuo Fu-jen, and his son. The enraged Kuo subsequently hanged himself. Sergeant Li was sentenced to 100 blows with the heavy bamboo, three years penal servitude, and to pay the survivors 10 ounces of silver, "by analogy to the sub-statute on innocent persons whose deaths result from undue punishment [torture] received in the course of judicial examination." Yin Kao-sheng, the soldier who actually beat Kuo, was sentenced to 80 blows of the heavy bamboo, as "provided by the statute on doing what ought not to be done," the famous "catch-all" provision of the Ch'ing code. Id. 458-60.

(3) In Honan province in 1888, a soldier who was under orders to execute a condemned prisoner (by strangulation) became drunk and improperly executed the sentence (by the more "heavy" punishment of decapitation), in violation of an imperial edict. The soldier was sentenced to 100 blows of the heavy bamboo and dismissal from the Army. Id. 474-75.

39. Ch'ing Dynasty penal code, supra note 31, § 220. The penalty of 100 blows and three years imprisonment could be increased to death by strangulation after two years imprisonment if the offender had communicated with foreign nations beyond the borders. Officers and guards who knew of the unauthorized border crossings, or who were not vigilant, could suffer similar penalties.

40. Id. § 202. Divulging military dispositions and plans to an enemy could bring death by beheading after two years imprisonment. Privately opening and reading any sealed government or official dispatch was

punishable by 60 blows; if the dispatch related to "any important military affairs," the punishment was increased to 100 blows and three years banishment "as a divulger of state secrets," even though the law states no requirement that the secrets be transmitted to another.

41. Id. § 212. The punishment was 40 blows if the article purchased was not "prohibited" (such as a weapon); purchasing prohibited articles could be punished by 80-100 blows and "perpetual banishment to a distance of 3,000 li."

42. Id. § 217. Punishable by 100 blows and military banishment.

43. Besides the cases summarized supra at note 38, the Peking Gazette, 25 April 1800, relates the case of an Army commissioner who converted military supplies to his own use, in violation of § 129, "Fraudulent Appropriation of Public Property" (this section falls under the Ch'ing code's Third Division, "Fiscal Laws," Book IV - "Public Property," rather than under the Fifth Division, "Military Laws"). 40 blows of the bamboo and life exile to Tartary was adjudged. A lieutenant "who connived at, and encouraged the corrupt practices of the said commissioner" was also given 40 blows, but kept in his regiment, "holding, however, one of [the] most laborious and least desirable situations in it, as a further mark of disgrace." Translated in Staunton, supra note 31, app. 16. In conformity with the Confucian practice of treating defendants differently based on class or social status, the Ch'ing code provides for slightly lighter punishments for "offenders of the Military Class" in certain cases (§ 10).

44. On the development of the legal system of the Republic of China, see generally Chiu & Fa, Law and Justice, in Contemporary Republic of

94

China 285 (J. Hsiung ed. 1981) and Chiu, _Legal Development in the Republic of China 1949-1981_, in China: Seventy Years After the 1911 Hsin-hai Revolution 287 (H. Chiu & S. Leng eds. 1984).

45. Chiu, _supra_ note 44, at 290.

46. _Id_. at 290-91.

47. _Id_. at 291; Rickett, _supra_ note 20.

48. Regulations Governing Military Criminal Cases (Promulgated by Presidential Mandate on March 26, 1915; Revised on April 17, 1918 and August 18, 1921), art. 1, in 1 _Legal and Political System in China_ 186-89 (H. Bhatia & T. Chung eds. 1974).

49. _Id_.

50. _Id_. art. 16.

51. "National People's Party" or Nationalists, the political party of Sun Yat-sen and subsequently Chiang Kai-shek.

52. Criminal Law of the Armed Forces, in _Compilation of the Laws of the Republic of China_ 503 (1967) [hereinafter _Compilation_].

53. Lee, _supra_ note 29, at 160.

54. _Compilation_, _supra_ note 52, at 497.

55. _Id_. at 539. On the operation of the ROC military legal system, _see generally_ Lee, _supra_ note 29; _see also_ Chiu & Fa and Chiu, _supra_ note

44, for its operations with respect to civilians under continuing martial law.

56. K. Marx & F. Engels, Manifesto of the Communist Party, ch. 2, in The Marx-Engels Reader 469, 487 (R. Tucker ed. 2d ed. 1978).

57. J. Hazard, Communists and their Law 69 (1969).

58. K. Marx, Critique of the Gotha Program, ch. 4, in R. Tucker, supra note 56, at 525, 538.

59. 1 E. H. Carr, The Bolshevik Revolution 155 (1985).

60. Id. at 141.

61. Id. at 156.

62. 33 V. Lenin Collected Works 221.

63. Mao, Report on the Investigation of the Peasant Movement, in Selected Readings from the Works of Mao Tsetung 30 (1971) [hereinafter Selected Readings].

64. On the People's Democratic Dictatorship, in Selected Readings, supra note 63, at 380.

65. Central Political-Judicial Cadre's School, Lectures on the General Principles of Criminal Law in the People's Republic of China 79, translated by Joint Publications Research Service [J.P.R.S.], No. 1331 (1962) [hereinafter Lectures].

66. Selected Readings, supra note 63, at 432.

67. Id. at 433-34.

68. Id.

69. Id. at 435-39.

70. Manifesto of the Third National Congress of the CCP, June 1923, in 1 W. Kuo, Analytical History of the Chinese Communist Party 151-52 (2d ed. 1968).

71. Mao, Problems of War and Strategy, in Selected Military Writings, supra note 6, at 269.

72. Clausewitz, On War 87 (Howard & Paret trans. 1984).

73. Quoted in Marxism-Leninism on War and Army 7 (Moscow 1972, U.S.A.F. reprint 1978). In Lenin's notes on Clausewitz he characterized Book 8, Chapter 6, entitled "War is an Instrument of Politics," as "the most important chapter"; his own summation of Clausewitz was "war is a part of a whole, and this whole is politics." Davis & Kohn, Lenin as Disciple of Clausewitz, Military Review, Sept. 1971, at 49, 50.

74. Mao, On Protracted War, in Selected Military Writings, supra note 6 at 187, 227.

75. Mao, supra note 71, at 274.

76. Id. at 275.

77. Comintern Instructions to CCP, in 10 J. Stalin Works 35 (1954).

78. Resolution on the Political Task and Policy of the CCP, August 1927, in Kuo, supra note 70, at 437, 449-50.

79. Mao, The Struggle in the Chingkang Mountains, in Selected Military Writings, supra note 6 at 21, 31-32.

80. Id. at 32.

81. Id. at 52 n.16.

82. Id.; in the 1950's, 90% of older officers, 30% of younger officers, and 10% of noncommissioned officers were CCP members. J. Guillermaz, The Chinese Communist Party in Power 1949-1976, at 163-65. More recently, "35% of the military have been accepted into the Party." F. Butterfield, China: Alive in the Bitter Sea 76 (1982).

83. Mao, On Correcting Mistaken Ideas in the Party, in Selected Military Writings, supra note 6 at 53, 54.

84. Id. at 56.

85. A Report on the History and Condition of the Chu-Mao Red Army, Sept. 1, 1929, in 6 Contemporary China 59, 73 (Kirby ed. 1968) [hereinafter Chu-Mao Report].

86. In requisitioning funds the Red Army was ordered to confiscate property, burn houses, and kill some of the local magnates as examples. Political Department of the Workers' and Peasants' Red

Army, 4th Division, "Brochure Concerning the Requisition of Funds," cited in Oda, Criminal Law and Procedure in the Chinese Soviet Republic, in The Legal System of the Chinese Soviet Republic 1931-1934, at 53 (W. Butler ed. 1983).

87. General Headquarters, Chinese People's Liberation Army (GHQ-CPLA), On the Reissue of the Three Main Rules of Discipline and the Eight Points for Attention, in Selected Military Writings, supra note 6 at 343, 344 n.1.

88. Id. While the Selected Military Writings editors credit Mao with these additions, Mao told Edgar Snow they were added by Lin Piao. Snow, supra note 27, at 176.

89. GHQ-CPLA, supra note 87, at 343. In relating the original rules to Edgar Snow, Mao omitted Points 7 and 8, substituting, "Be honest in all transactions with the peasants," and "Be sanitary, and especially establish latrines a safe distance from people's homes." Point 3 was expanded: "Be courteous and polite to the people and help them when you can." Snow, supra note 27, at 176. In 1937 Mao listed Disciplinary Rule 3 as "Be neither selfish nor unjust." Mao, On Guerrilla Warfare 92 (Griffith trans. 1961). Mao probably did not wish to offend Nationalist sensibilities by using the original version and its endorsement of expropriations during the United Front then prevailing for the war with Japan.

90. GHQ-CPLA, supra note 87, at 343.

91. See infra note 312 and accompanying text.

92. The code was not only frequently recited, but also sung daily in a Red Army marching song. Snow, supra note 27, at 176. The code, together with its underlying political purposes, was part of the basic political training of new Red Army soldiers. Resolution of the Ninth CCP Congress of the Red Fourth Army, Dec. 1929 [hereinafter Resolution], in 2 Collected Works of Mao Tse-tung, 1917-1949 at 165, 186, 189, translated by Joint Publications Research Service No. 71911 (1978) [hereinafter Collected Works].

93. In On Guerrilla Warfare Mao listed this code as a factor in achieving a "unity of spirit" that should exist between the people and the troops. "The former may be likened to water and the latter to the fish who inhabit it....". It is only undisciplined troops who make the people their enemies and who, like the fish out of its native element, cannot live." Mao, supra note 89, at 92-93.

94. Resolution, supra note 92, at 182.

95. Id. at 185.

96. Chu-Mao Report, supra note 85, at 72-73. Although corporal punishment was permitted under these penal rules, Mao considered the practice a remnant from feudal warlords and a "monstrosity." Mao advocated the abolition of corporal punishment as an enhancement to morale, and called for the Red Army penal regulations to be revised. Resolution, supra note 92, at 190-92. The practice evidently remains a problem in the PLA; the new "Eight Prohibitions," proposed in August 1986 as a supplement to the Three Main Rules of Discipline and Eight Points for Attention, proscribe corporal punishment in the first "prohibition." See infra text accompanying note 419.

97. For legal developments during the CSR period see generally S. Leng, Justice in Communist China 1-10 (1967), T. Lotveit, Chinese Communism 1931-1934 ch. 5 (1973), and The Legal System of the Chinese Soviet Republic 1931-1934 (W. Butler ed. 1983) [hereinafter Butler].

98. Resolution of the All-China Congress of Soviets Concerning the Red Army, November 1931, in Fundamental Laws of the Chinese Soviet Republic 35-36 (N.Y.: International, 1934).

99. Id.

100. Id. at 39-43.

101. Id. at 45.

102. Provisional Procedure for Deciding Cases on Counter-Revolutionary Crimes and Instituting Judicial Organs, 13 Dec. 1931 (Directive No. 6 of CEC-CSR), in Butler, supra note 97, app. 19.

103. Id. See generally P. Griffin, The Chinese Communist Treatment of Counterrevolutionaries: 1924-1949 (1976).

104. 2 Kuo, supra note 70, at 285; Lotveit, supra note 97, at 115; Oda, supra note 86, at 59.

105. Organic Program of the State Political Security Bureau of the Chinese Soviet Republic, in Butler, supra note 97, app. 18, art. 10.

106. Id.

107. Id. art. 5.

108. Id. art. 8.

109. Translation at infra app. 3 [hereinafter Military Courts Organizational Regulations]. Original in Shih-sou tzu-liao-shih kung-fei tzu-liao (Hoover Institution, microfilm, 1960) no. 008.5524/3754/0553, reel 7, item 15. A Russian translation of these regulations, subsequently translated into English, is in Butler, supra note 97, app. 17.

110. See infra chapter V. These are the only known organizational regulations for Chinese Communist military courts. See infra text accompanying notes 192-93 & 284-85.

111. Military Courts Organizational Regulations, supra note 109, arts. 4-7. The incorporation of the military courts into the overall CSR judicial system is reflected in the Organic Law of the Central Soviet, Feb. 17, 1934, in 4 Collected Works, supra note 92, at 225. The military courts, civil courts and criminal courts were all established under the Supreme Court (art. 36), which was to review decisions of the provincial and higher military courts (art. 37). No pretense of judicial independence was made; the Supreme Court was subject to the CSR Central Executive Comittee (art. 34). The CEC periodically reviewed and revised Supreme Court decisions. See Resolution on the Conviction of Important Military Criminals of the Reformed Faction of the AB Group by the Provisional Supreme Court, Feb. 1932, in 3 Collected Works, supra note 92, at 67.

112. Military Courts Organizational Regulations, art. 2.

113. Id. art 1. Neither a criminal law nor a military criminal law was ever enacted by the CSR, although enactment of a criminal law was proposed in 1933. See Oda, supra note 86, at 67. The PRC finally enacted a criminal law in 1978, and a military criminal law in 1981.

114. Military Courts Organizational Regulations art. 1.

115. Id. arts. 12, 13. The use of assessors (also called lay judges or jurors), who were elected from among the officers and soldiers (or from Party organizations for civilian courts), was borrowed from the Soviet Union. This regulation is the first Chinese Communist enactment to mention them. Their primary function was to educate the masses concerning law and judicial procedures. Assessors were to be relieved of other military duties for their one-week term.

116. Id. art. 12.

117. Id. arts. 18, 20.

118. Id. art. 21.

119. Id. arts. 27, 28.

120. Id. art. 24.

121. Provisional Rules on the Organization of Judicial Sections and Court Procedure, 9 June 1932, in Butler, supra note 97, app. 15 [hereinafter Provisional Court Procedure].

122. On the Question of Suppressing Internal Counterrevolution, 15 Mar. 1933 (Directive No. 21 of CEC-CSR), in 3 Collected Works, supra note 92, at 154.

123. Provisional Court Procedure, supra note 121, art. 26. Article 21 of the Military Courts Organizational Regulations contained a similar requirement for review of death sentences, but a note thereto allowed execution with subsequent confirmation "under extraordinary military conditions." See infra app. 3, art. 21.

124. On Strict Control of Departing Persons, 27 Dec. 1932 (Order No. 37 of CEC-CSR), in 3 Collected Works, supra note 92, at 134.

125. P. Griffin, supra note 103, at 59.

126. Id.

127. On the AWOL Problem in the Red Army, 15 Dec. 1933 (Order No. 25 of CEC-CSR), in 4 Collected Works, supra note 92, at 86.

128. Id.

129. See supra text accompanying note 100.

130. P. Griffin, supra note 103, at 61.

131. Chang complained that judicial personnel did not understand "that the soviet laws are produced to meet the demands of the struggle against counter-revolution, and they are not made in order to serve as a basis for extenuating the crimes of the counter-revolutionaries." He criticized the earlier system of reviewing death sentences as "letting

the enthusiastic demands of the masses be cooled off by the many 'approvals,' and causing the effect of the executions of counter-revolutionaries in inciting the struggle of the masses, and in educating the masses, to be very badly weakened." Tou-Cheng No. 49, at 6, 7, quoted in Lotveit, supra note 97, at 125, 140.

132.   Decree No. 5, CEC-CSR, 9 Feb. 1934, quoted in T. Lotveit, supra note 97, at 122.

133.   Liang Po-t'ai, The Main Line of the Judicial Organs: Suppress the Counter-Revolution, Hung-se Chung-hua, Mar. 1, 1934, at 3, quoted in T. Lotveit, supra note 97, at 140.

134.   Judicial Procedure of the Chinese Soviet Republic, 8 Apr. 1934, in 4 Collected Works, supra note 92, at 240-42. Also translated in Butler, supra note 97, app. 16 [hereinafter Judicial Procedure].

135.   Statute of the Chinese Soviet Republic Governing the Punishment of Counterrevolutionaries, 8 Apr. 1934, in 4 Collected Works, supra note 92, at 243-48. Also translated in Butler, supra note 97, app. 20, and in P. Griffin, supra note 103, app. B [hereinafter CSR Statute on Counterrevolutionaries].

136.   Judicial Procedure, supra note 134, art. 3. This authority was also granted to provincial and hsien judicial sections, and to local committees for the eradication of counterrevolutionaries.

137.   Id. art. 5.

138.   Id. art. 6.

139. CSR Statute on Counterrevolutionaries, _supra_ note 135, art. 16.

140. _Id._ arts. 19, 20, 21, 15, and 13.

141. See _supra_ text accompanying note 102.

142. Constitution of the Chinese Soviet Republic, 7 Nov. 1931, in C. Brandt, B. Schwartz and J. Fairbank, _A Documentary History of Chinese Communism_ 220-24 (1952), art. 1.

143. _Id._ art. 4.

144. _Id._ art. 2.

145. See _supra_ note 102.

146. Organic Program of the SPSB, _supra_ note 105, art. 11.

147. CSR Statute on Counterrevolutionaries, _supra_ note 135, art. 34: "Worker and peasant criminals who are not leaders, or whose crimes are not serious, should be given lighter sentences than those of the landlord bourgeoisie, in accordance with the stipulation of these articles." Art. 35: "For those who rendered meritorious service to the Soviet, sentences for their crimes should be lightened, in accordance with the stipulations carried in the articles."

148. Judicial Procedure, _supra_ note 134, art. 5.

149. Report of the Central Executive Committee and the People's Committee of the CSR to the Second All-Soviet Congress, 23 Jan. 1934, in 4 Collected Works _supra_ note 92, at 155, 175.

150. Organic Program of the SPSB, supra note 105, art. 11; CSR Statute on Counterrevolutionaries, supra note 135, art. 36.

151. See supra text accompanying notes 46 & 47.

152. R. Makepeace, Marxist Ideology and Soviet Criminal Law 105 (1980).

153. Id. at 71, 72.

154. Id. at 106. The doctrine was finally eliminated in the 1960 RSFSR Criminal Code.

155. CCP Anti-Japanese Declaration for National Salvation, Nov. 28, 1935, in 5 Collected Works, supra note 92, at 1.

156. The CCP's Public Statement on KMT-CCP Co-operation, Sept. 22, 1937, in C. Brandt, B. Schwartz and J. Fairbank, supra note 142, at 245-47.

157. 3 Kuo, supra note 70, at 292.

158. Id.

159. Mao, Interview with the British Journalist James Bertram, Oct. 25, 1937, in 2 Selected Works of Mao Tse-tung 53 (1965).

160. Revised Laws Governing Emergency Crimes Endangering the Republic, Sept. 4, 1937, reissued Feb. 10, 1938 by the Shansi-Chahar-Hopei Border Region Administrative Committee, in P. Griffin, supra note 103, app. J.

161. Revised Statute Concerning Punishment of Traitors, Oct. 15, 1938, in P. Griffin, supra note 103, app. K.

162. Draft Statute of the Shensi-Kansu-Ninghsia Border Region Concerning Martial Law During War, 1939, in P. Griffin, supra note 103, app. E.

163. Draft Statute of the Shensi-Kansu-Ninghsia Border Region Governing Punishment of Traitors During War Times, 1939, in P. Griffin, supra note 103, app. D.

164. The Shensi-Kansu-Ninghsia Border Region Statute Protecting Human and Propery Rights, Feb. 1942, in P. Griffin, supra note 103, app. C.

165. P. Griffin, supra note 103, at 91-92, quoting A. Smedley, Battle Hymn of China 483 (1943).

166. Quoted in S. Leng, supra note 97, at 23.

167. Military Court of the Anhui Provincial Military District, Strengthening the Legal System in the Military to Ensure Victory in War, translated in Foreign Broadcast Information Service, People's Republic of China Daily Report [F.B.I.S.], July 13, 1981, at O1.

168. The Common Program of the Chinese People's Political Consultative Conference, Sept. 29, 1949, in Fundamental Legal Documents of Communist China 34 (A. Blaustein ed. 1962).

169. Chieh-fang Jih-Pao (Liberation Daily), Shanghai, June 6, 7, and 16, 1949, translated in A. Rickett, Legal Thought and Institutions of the People's Republic of China: Selected Documents 213-19 (U. Pa. Inst. for Legal Res., mimeographed, 1964).

170. Id. at 218.

171. Statute on Penalties for Corruption in the Chinese People's Republic, Apr. 21, 1952, in Blaustein, supra note 168, at 227.

172. Statute on Punishment for Counterrevolutionary Activity, Feb. 20, 1951, in Blaustein, supra note 168, at 215 [hereinafter PRC Statute on Counterrevolutionaries].

173. Provisional Regulations for the Preservation of State Secrets, June 8, 1951, in 2 China L. Rep. 274-78, art. 2 (1983).

174. See generally Organization Regulations of People's Tribunals, translated in Current Background (Hong Kong: U.S. Consulate General), No. 151, Jan. 10, 1952.

175. Mao admitted that 800,000 "enemies of the people" had been "liquidated" up to 1954 in the unedited version of his 1957 speech "On the Correct Handling of Contradictions Among the People." Cohen, supra note 9, at 10 n.17. A French authority has estimated that five million Chinese were executed between 1949 and 1952. Guillermaz, supra note 82, at 24 n.8. The Nationalist Chinese claim the 1949-1952 toll was 19.3 million killed. Ministry of Justice Investigation Bureau, 2 The Charts of the Existing Conditions of the Chinese Communists 34 (1972). In June 1957 Premier Chou En-lai reported to the National People's Congress that 16.8% of counterrevolutionaries tried had been

sentenced to death and 42.3% had been sentenced to reform through labor, with the remainder receiving administrative punishments. Amnesty International, Political Imprisonment in the People's Republic of China 29 (1978).

176. Mao, Comments on the Work of Suppressing and Liquidating Counterrevolutionaries, June 15, 1951, in Miscellany of Mao Tse-tung Thought (1949-1968) pt. 1, at 6, 8 (Joint Publications Research Service [J.P.R.S.] No. 61269-1, Feb. 20, 1974).

177. Resolutions of Third National Conference on Public Security, May 15, 1951, in id. at 9, 10.

178. Jen-min Jih-pao (People's Daily), June 3, 1950, cited in T. Hsia, Guide to Selected Legal Sources of Mainland China 12 (1967).

179. Jen-min Jih-pao, Aug. 25, 1951, cited in L. Gudoshnikov, Legal Organs of the People's Republic of China (Moscow 1957), translated in J.P.R.S. No. 1698, at 79.

180. PRC Statute on Counterrevolutionaries, supra note 172, art. 20: "The affairs of persons who have committed crimes specified in this Statute while military administrative committees are functioning are subject to consideration by military tribunals set up by the headquarters of military districts, military administrative committees, or organizations combatting banditry."

181. The Trial and Conviction of U.S. Spies in Peking: Texts of the Indictment and Verdict, People's China (Supplement), Sept. 1, 1951.

182. Id. at 3.

183. See supra note 180.

184. U.S. Spy Ring Smashed in Peking, People's China, Sept. 1, 1951, at 25, 27.

185. Constitution of the People's Republic of China, Sept. 20, 1954, in Blaustein, supra note 168, at 1-33 [hereinafter Constitution (1954)].

186. Constitution (Fundamental Law) of the Union of Soviet Socialist Republics, 1936, arts. 112, 123, in The Soviet Legal System 61-79 (W. Butler comp. 1978). See generally Cohen, China's Changing Constitution, 1 Nw. J. Int'l L. & Bus. 57 (1979).

187. Lectures, supra note 65, at 189.

188. See generally Regulations on Active Service of CPLA Officers, Feb. 8, 1955, translated in Current Background No. 312, Feb. 15, 1955.

189. See generally Military Service Law, July 30, 1955, translated in Current Background No. 344, Aug. 8, 1955, at 4-11. A new version of the Military Service Law was enacted May 31, 1984, translated in F.B.I.S., June 6, 1984, at K1.

190. Organic Law of the People's Courts of the PRC, Sept. 21, 1954, in Blaustein, supra note 168, at 131.

191. Organic Law of the People's Procuratorates of the PRC, Sept. 21, 1954, in Blaustein, supra note 168, at 144.

192. Organic Law of the People's Courts, art. 27; Organic Law of the People's Procuratorates, art. 1.

193. T. Hsia, supra note 178, at 12.

194. New China News Agency, PLA Revives Military Courts, Procuratorates, Dec. 6, 1978, translated in F.B.I.S., Dec. 8, 1978, at E21.

195. Id.

196. T. Hsia, supra note 178, at 12.

197. Id.

198. Yang, Organization of Military Regions and Power Seizure, Chinese Communist Affairs, Oct. 1967, at 48.

199. Code of Military Discipline of the Chinese People's Liberation Army, Nov. 25, 1975, art. 3, translated in Issues & Studies, Oct. 1976, at 89,90 [hereinafter PLA Discipline Regulation (1975)].

200. Regulations on Active Service of CPLA Officers, supra note 188, art 4.

201. Military Court of the Anhui Provincial Military District, supra note 167, at O1.

202. See supra text accompanying notes 171 & 172.

203. Two Documents From the CCP CC Military Commission, Issues & Studies, Oct. 1976, at 88, editor's note.

204. Handbook on the Chinese Armed Forces p. 5-28 (U.S. Defense Intelligence Agency 1976).

205. Judgment on U.S. Espionage Cases, People's China (Supplement), Dec. 16, 1954.

206. See supra text accompanying notes 181-84.

207. Article 76 of the 1954 Constitution guaranteed an accused the right to defense.

208. This practice is codified in Article 14 of the Statute on Punishing Counterrevolutionaries: Persons who have committed crimes specified in this Statute may be treated leniently, their punishment may be mitigated or may be completely exempted from punishment if one of the following circumstances obtains:

> (1) They voluntarily appear before the people's government; admit their guilt, and sincerely repent of their crimes;
> (2) Before the discovery or investigation of a crime or after it they frankly confess to what they have done and are sincerely repentant and by their selfless work atone for the crime. . . .

209. See supra text accompanying note 172.

210. Regulations on PLA Political Work, 1963, I.3, quoted in H. Jencks, From Muskets to Missiles: Politics and Professionalism in the Chinese Army, 1945-1981, at 236 (1982).

211. Id. at 240. Political Commissars regularly received instructions on how to administer discipline in their units. Commissars at the regimental level received a weekly "Bulletin of Activities" from the PLA General Political Department, classified "secret." As an example, Bulletin 13 (Mar. 20, 1961) reported three cases of soldiers who committed suicide due to inadequate handling of discipline by political officers and commanders. Translated in The Politics of the Chinese Red Army: A Translation of the Bulletin of Activities of the P.L.A. 356-59 (J. Cheng ed. 1966).

212. Political and Legal Work Research Group, Department of Law, People's University of China, Several Problems Relating to the Legal System of the Chinese People's Democracy, Cheng-fa Yen-chiu (Political and Judicial Study), Apr. 1959, at 3-8, translated in A. Rickett, supra note 169, at 9, 12.

213. Id. at 10, 11.

214. Id. at 11.

215. According to the indictment of the trial of the Gang of Four (Nov. 1980-Jan. 1981), a total of 729,511 people (including over 80,000 PLA members) were allegedly framed and persecuted in the years 1966-1976, of whom more than 34,800 (including 1,169 PLA members) were persecuted to death. A Great Trial in Chinese History 20-21, 173-184 (1981). Agence France-Press estimated that 400,000 to 800,000 were killed from 1966 to 1969. Butterfield, supra note 82, at 348-49. The

114

Nationalist Chinese claim two million were killed from 1966 to 1970. Ministry of Justice Investigation Bureau, supra note 175, at 34.

216. Translated in Survey of China Mainland Press [SCMP] (Hong Kong: U.S. Consulate General), No. 3879, Feb. 14, 1967, at 13.

217. Completely Smash the Feudal, Capitalist and Revisionist Legal Systems, Survey of China Mainland Magazines [SCMM] (Hong Kong: U.S. Consulate General), No. 625, Sept. 3, 1968, at 23.

218. Id. at 24, 25.

219. Id. at 27. The provision for judicial independence in Art. 78 of the 1954 Constitution was omitted from the Maoists' 1975 Constitution.

220. Id. at 23, 24. The Maoists called for a strict class interpretation of law: "Law is one of the weapons used to curb the sabotage activities of the class enemies, and is strong in class character. The mastery of law by the proletariat is for the purpose of defending its state power. Because of this, law must be commanded by the Party like the gun, and can never be allowed to dominate the Party. Id. at 28.

221. Quoted in Leng, supra note 11, at 359.

222. T. Hsia and K. Haun, The Re-Emergence of the Procuratorial System in the People's Republic of China, 20-27 (Library of Congress Far Eastern Law Division 1978).

223. Decision of the CCPCC on Resolute Support for the Revolutionary Masses of the Left, Jan. 23, 1967, Current Background No. 852, May 6, 1968, at 49.

224. Order of the Military Commission of the Central Committee, Jan. 28, 1967, Current Background No. 852, May 6, 1968, at 54.

225. Proclamation of the PRC Ministry of Public Security and the PLA Peking Garrison Headquarters, Feb. 11, 1967, Current Background No. 852, May 6, 1968, at 67.

226. Bulletin of the PLA Military Control Commission of the Peking Municipal Public Security Bureau, Feb. 25, 1967, in Chinese L. & Gov't, Fall/Winter 1971-72, at 328.

227. Vice Premier Hsieh Fu-chih's Talk at the Supreme People's Court, Feb. 16, 1967, S.C.M.P. No. 4157, 1968, at 4. Several of the Supreme Court members were subsequently persecuted and expelled from the CCP. L. Tao, Criminal Justice in Communist China (pt. 2), Issues & Studies, July 1977, at 19, 48. In 1969 the court members were "sent down" to work in the fields of Hubei province. They were not allowed to return to Peking until after 1973. J. Tao, La Cour Populaire Supreme de la Republique Populaire de Chine, 37 Revue Internationale de Droit Compare 107, 111 (1985).

228. Some Directives Concerning the Dispatching of the "Central Support-the-Left" Units in All Military Regions and Provincial Military Districts, June 10, 1968, in Chinese L. & Gov't, Fall/Winter 1971-72, at 330, 332.

229. The July 23 [1969] Proclamation, in Chinese L. & Gov't, Fall/Winter 1970-71, at 269, 271.

230. Constitution of the Communist Party of China, Aug. 28, 1973, art. 7, in The Tenth National Congress of the CCP (Documents) 61, 69 (1973).

231. Constitution of the People's Republic of China, Jan. 17, 1975, arts. 2, 15 [hereinafter Constitution (1975)], in T. Hsia and K. Haun, The 1975 Revised Constitution of the People's Republic of China, app. B (Library of Congress Far Eastern Law Division 1975). See generally The New Constitution of Communist China (M. Lindsay ed. 1976).

232. Leng, supra note 11, at 360.

233. Chiu, The Judicial System Under the New PRC Constitution, in Lindsay, supra note 231, at 89 n.87.

234. Hsia, The Tenth Party Congress and the Future Development of Law in China, in House Comm. on Foreign Affairs, Oil and Asian Rivals, Sino-Soviet Conflict - Japan and the Oil Crisis, Hearings before Subcomm. on Asian and Pacific Affairs, 93d Cong., 1st & 2d Sess. 379, 404 (1973-74).

235. A number of military control committee sentencing documents are analyzed in Chiu, Criminal Punishment in Mainland China: A Study of Some Yunnan Province Documents, 68 J. of Crim. L. & Criminology 374 (1977), and in Edwards, Reflections on Crime and Punishment in China, With Appended Sentencing Documents, 16 Colum. J. Transnat'l L. 45 (1977).

236. Notice of the CPLA Military Control Committee (Section) of the Public Security Organ, the Procuratorial Organ, and the Court of Ching-hung County, Hsi-hsuan-pan-na Chou, Jan. 26, 1971, in Chiu,

supra note 235, at 393, doc. 2 [hereinafter PLA MCC Notice, Jan. 26, 1971].

237. Control, the lowest criminal penalty imposed by the courts, is a form of supervised labor where the offender remains in society under surveillance. See the listing of informal, administrative, and criminal penalties in Amnesty International, supra note 175, at 57, 58.

238. PLA MCC Notice, Jan. 26, 1971, supra note 236, at 394.

239. Notice of the CPLA Military Control Committee of the Public Security Organs of the Szu-Mao Region of Yunnan Province, Feb. 11, 1972, in Edwards, supra note 235, at 97, doc. C.

240. Adultery or cohabitation with the spouse of a PLA member has long been a criminal offense, although adultery per se is not. The violator here was sentenced to 3 years imprisonment, which is the maximum penalty for this offense under the subsequently-enacted Criminal Law of the People's Republic of China, art. 181 (1979), translated in 73 J. Crim. L & Criminology 138.

241. Notice of the CPLA Military Control Section of the Public Security Organs of Meng-lien County, Yunnan Province, Aug. 8, 1972, in Edwards, supra note 235, at 93, doc. B.

242. New China News Agency, supra note 194, at E21.

243. People's Liberation Army Code of Interior Management, Nov. 25, 1975, art. 3 [hereinafter PLA Internal Administration Regulation], translated in Issues & Studies, Oct. 1976, at 98.

244. PLA Discipline Regulation (1975), supra note 199, art. 4.

245. See supra notes 199 & 243. For example, Article 3 of the Disciplinary Regulation declared: "Theories of Marxism, Leninism, and Mao Tse-tung Thought concerning dictatorship of the proletariat and Chairman Mao's line of army-building are the guidelines for maintaining and consolidating the discipline of our army." Similarly, Article 2 of the Internal Administration Regulation proclaimed: "Correctness of ideological and political line determines everything."

246. See supra text accompanying notes 66-69.

247. Mao, On the Ten Great Relationships, Apr. 25, 1956, in Chairman Mao Talks to the People 61, 78 (S. Schram ed. 1974). Mao suggested that, rather than executing these offenders, they should undergo "labor reform, so that rubbish can be transformed into something useful. Besides, people's heads are not like leeks. When you cut them off, they will not grow again. If you cut a head off wrongly, there is no way of rectifying the mistake even if you want to." Id. at 78.

248. See supra note 75 and accompanying text.

249. The New Republic, May 22, 1979, at 9, quoted in Chinese L. & Gov't, Winter 1970-71, at 271.

250. Leading Maoists led by Mao's widow, Jiang Qing. See generally Symposium: The Trial of the "Gang of Four" and its Implication in China (J. Hsiung ed. U. Md. Sch. L. Occasional Papers/Reprints Series in Contemporary Asian Studies No. 3-1981(40)).

251. Publicizing the New Laws, Beijing Review, July 20, 1979, at 4.

252. Constitution of the People's Republic of China, Mar. 5, 1978, in Documents of the First Session of the Fifth National People's Congress of the People's Republic of China 125-72 (1978) [hereinafter Constitution (1978)]. One of the Maoist features remaining in the 1978 Constitution was the retention of the CCPCC Chairman as commander of the PLA (art. 19); added was a citizen's duty to support the Party (art. 56). See generally Cohen, supra note 186 for a comparative analysis of the 1954, 1975, and 1978 Constitutions.

253. Constitution (1978), art. 41.

254. Id. art. 43. See generally T. Hsia and K. Haun, supra n.222.

255. T. Hsia & K. Haun, Peking's Minister of Public Security on Strengthening the Legal System 47-56 (Library of Congress Far Eastern Law Division 1979).

256. Communique of the Third Plenary Session of the 11th Central Committee of the Communist Party of China, Peking Review, Dec. 29, 1978, at 14.

257. The Criminal Law of the People's Republic of China, July 1, 1979, translated in 73 J. Crim. L. & Criminology 138 [hereinafter Criminal Law].

258. The Criminal Procedure Law of the People's Republic of China, July 1, 1979, translated in 73 J. Crim. L. & Criminology 171 [hereinafter Criminal Procedure Law].

259. The Law on the Organization of the People's Courts of the People's Republic of China, translated in The Criminal Procedure Code of the PRC and Related Documents 84 (C. Kim ed. 1985).

260. The Law on the Organization of the People's Procuratorates of the People's Republic of China, translated in Kim, supra note 259, at 96.

261. S. Leng & H. Chiu, Criminal Justice in Post-Mao China 40 (1985).

262. Constitution of the People's Republic of China, Dec. 4, 1982, translated in Beijing Review, Dec. 27, 1982, at 10-29 [hereinafter Constitution (1982)]. See generally Chiu, The 1982 Chinese Constitution and the Rule of Law, 11 Rev. Socialist L. 143 (1985).

263. See supra note 252.

264. S. Leng & H. Chiu, supra note 261, at 53.

265. Constitution (1982) supra note 262, at 11, Preamble.

266. New China News Agency, supra note 194, at E21-22.

267. Id. at E22.

268. Shanghai City Service, Shanghai Military Courts Restored, Feb. 25, 1980, translated in F.B.I.S., Feb. 29, 1980, at O4.

269. Peking Domestic Service, Open PLA Military Court Sentences Army Cadres, Dec. 7, 1978, translated in F.B.I.S., Dec. 8, 1978, at E22-23.

270. Beijing Domestic Service, PLA Military Procuratorate Reestablished, Holds First Conference, Mar. 20, 1979, translated in F.B.I.S., Mar. 21, 1979, at L20-21.

271. Id. For text of the Arrest and Detention Act of the PRC, Feb. 23, 1979, see S. Leng & H. Chiu, supra note 261, at 187, doc. 3.

272. Beijing Domestic Service, supra note 270, at L21. That military procurators and other legal workers continue to require encouragement to carry out their duties despite corruption and arbitrary superiors is evident from an article concerning military law enforcment during the Western Han Dynasty, published in Guangming Ribao on Nov. 7, 1984, at 3. Apparently a parable to be applied currently, the article praises the ancient incorruptible military law executioner Hu Jian for enforcing the law strictly, alertly and calmly, "without deferring to the high and mighty." Hu executed a corrupt Imperial inspector under military law, although the inspector was a civilian. The Emperor excused this by decreeing that since the violations of the law occurred in an army camp, military law was applicable. The moral of the parable appears to lie in Hu's written memorial to the throne: "It is said that military law is indispensible in the Army because it aims at building the power and prestige of the Army so that all Army officers and fighters may be in awe of it, and that punishment of those evildoers who have undermined the Army will inspire the Army." Liao Zhi, Hu Jian Enforced the Law Without Deferring to the High and Mighty - A Story of Law Enforcement in Ancient Times, translated in F.B.I.S., Nov. 15, 1984, at K9-11.

273. Xinhua News Agency, Presidents of People's Courts, Military Tribunals Meet, Aug. 2, 1979, translated in F.B.I.S., Aug. 2, 1979 at L12-13.

274. National judicial training classes for military officers transferred to judicial work, Law Annual Report of China 1982/3, at 210, 211 (Hong Kong: Kingsway, 1982).

275. Xinhua News Agency, Cadres Being Trained Throughout China to Publicize New Laws, Aug. 2, 1979, translated in F.B.I.S., Aug. 2, 1979, at L13.

276. Kunming Yunnan Provincial Service, Yunnan PLA Units Organize Legal Training Course, Jan. 18, 1980, translated in F.B.I.S., Jan. 22, 1980, at Q5.

277. Xinhua News Agency, PLA Launches 3-Year Legal Education Program, July 25, 1986, translated in F.B.I.S., July 25, 1986, at K9.

278. Beijing Domestic Service, Legal Knowledge Circular, Dec. 11, 1985, translated in Joint Publications Research Service, China Report: Political, Sociological, and Military Affairs, Jan. 7, 1986, at 122 [hereinafter JPRS-CPS]. Pedagogical techniques used in past PLA legal publicity campaigns include slide shows, films, bulletin boards, discussions, and courses. Ai Pu & Ji Juxing, Guangzhou Military Region Conducts Legal System Publicity and Education Activities, Renmin Ribao, May 13, 1985, translated in JPRS-CPS, June 7, 1985, at 134, 135. Courses study the PRC Constitution, Criminal Law, Military Service Law, Military Criminal Law, and a number of civil laws. The studies are to assist PLA members to "get rid of such erroneous concepts as 'power instead of law,' 'punishment in place of

law,' and 'personal feelings taking precedence of law' which existed in their minds to one extent or another." The courses include a final examination. Xinhua News Agency, Shenyang Military Region Leaders Take Legal Exam, Apr. 24, 1986, translated in JPRS-CPS, May 27, 1986, at 85.

279. Constitution (1982), art. 124: "The People's Republic of China establishes the Supreme People's Court and the local people's courts at different levels, military courts and other special courts."

280. Organic Law of the People's Courts, supra note 259, art. 2: "The judicial authority of the PRC is exercised by the following people's courts: . . . (2) military courts and other special courts (as amended 1983. S. Leng & H. Chiu, supra note 261, at 65 n.19).

281. Id. art. 3.

282. Constitution (1984), art. 130: "The People's Republic of China establishes the Supreme People's Procuratorate and the local people's procuratorates at different levels, military procuratorates and other special procuratorates."

283. Organic Law of the People's Procuratorates, supra note 260, art. 2.

284. Organic Law of the People's Courts, art. 29; Organic Law of the People's Procuratorates, art. 2.

285. Tsien, supra note 2, at 182.

286. Each of the two criminal divisions is composed of three sections; each section corresponds to two administrative regions which existed before the Cultural Revolution. Each division thus includes a section for east and southwest China, a section for north and northeast China, and a section for northwest and south-central China. Military cases are assigned to the sections for east and southwest China. J. Tao, supra note 227, at 121.

287. Law Annual Report of China, supra note 274, at 50, 51.

288. Id. at 48, 49. The power to appoint or remove the President of the Military Court or the Chief Procurator of the Military Procuratorate is vested in the Standing Committee of the National People's Congress, at the suggestion of the President of the Supreme People's Court or the Procurator-General of the Supreme People's Procuratorate, respectively. Constitution (1982), art. 67(11), (12).

289. Tsien, supra note 2, at 182.

290. Id.

291. Barlow & Wagner, "Public Order and Internal Security," in China: A Country Study 425, 439 (Bunge & Shinn eds., Dep't of the Army Pamphlet 550-60, 1981).

292. Tsien, supra note 2, at 182.

293. Criminal Law, supra note 257.

294. Id. art 2.

295. Id. pt. 2, chs. 1-8, arts. 90-192.

296. Id. pt. 1, ch. 3, arts. 27-56.

297. Id. art. 9.

298. Criminal Procedure Law, supra note 258, art. 31.

299. Id. art. 32.

300. Id. art. 35.

301. Criminal Law art. 63.

302. Id. art. 79: "A crime that is not expressly provided for in the Special Provisions of this Law may be determined and punished by reference to the most closely analogous article of the Special Provisions of this Law, but the matter must be submitted to the Supreme People's Court for approval."

303. Anhui Military Court, supra note 167, at O2.

304. Xinhua News Agency, Explanation of Regulations, June 10, 1981, translated in F.B.I.S., June 12, 1981, at K4.

305. See infra app. 1. Chinese text in 12 State Council Bulletin (1981), translation in F.B.I.S., June 12, 1981, at K1 [hereinafter Military Criminal Law].

306. Explanation of Regulations, supra note 304, at K4.

307. Military Criminal Law, art. 23.

308. Explanation of Regulations, supra note 304, at K5.

309. See infra sec. V.C.1.

310. Explanation of Regulations, supra note 304, at K4.

311. Id.

312. People's Liberation Army Discipline Regulation, Jan. 27, 1984, translated infra app. 2. Chinese text in 1985 Yearbook on Chinese Communism 9-15 to 9-22 (Taipei 1985) [hereinafter PLA Discipline Regulation (1984)]. The 1984 Regulation, classified as a state military secret in the PRC, superseded the 1975 version (supra note 199), which in turn superseded the 1963 version. Two Documents from the CCPCC Military Commission, supra note 203, editor's note.

313. PLA Discipline Regulation (1984) art. 2.

314. Id. ch. 2; PLA Discipline Regulation (1975) art. 6. The three classes of medals of merit are illustrated in Handbook of the Chinese People's Liberation Army 93 (U.S. Defense Intelligence Agency 1984).

315. PLA Discipline Regulation (1984) art. 20.

316. Id. art. 21.

317. Id. art. 22.

318. Id. art. 22(1), (2).

319. PLA Internal Administration Regulation, supra note 243. This regulation was revised in Sep. 1984 and expanded from 71 to 163 articles, but is as yet unavailable in English. Chinese text in 1985 Yearbook on Chinese Communism 9-22 to 9-43 (Taipei 1985).

320. Provisional Regulations for the Preservation of State Secrets, supra note 173. The regulations were reissued in April 1980. F.B.I.S., Apr. 14, 1980, at L7.

321. Cheng, supra note 211, at 236. A draft text of the third amendment and supplement of these classified regulations was circulated to political commissars in Feb. 1961, and appears in id. at 236-243.

322. New China News Agency, Military Commission Issues Documents on Security, May 20, 1978, translated in F.B.I.S., May 22, 1978, at E1.

323. Regulation on PLA Safeguarding of State and Military Secrets, 1978, quoted in id. at E1. These rules are also incorporated in the 1984 PLA Internal Administration Regulation, supra note 319, at app. 4.

324. PLA Discipline Regulation (1984) art. 22(6).

325. Military Criminal Law art. 4.

326. Criminal Law art. 186.

327. See text accompanying notes 210-11.

328. PLA Internal Administration Regulation art. 15.

329. PLA Discipline Regulation (1984) arts 4, 23, 24.

330. Id. art. 22.

331. Handbook of the Chinese People's Liberation Army, supra note 314, at 17; Amnesty International, supra note 175, at 57.

332. Amnesty International, supra note 175, at 57.

333. PLA Discipline Regulation (1984) art. 32.

334. Id. art. 29.

335. Id. art. 30.

336. Id. art. 36.

337. Id. art. 29.

338. Id. art. 32.

339. Id. art. 31.

340. Id. art. 38.

341. Id. art. 37.

342. Id. art. 35.

343. Id. art. 22 (15).

344. Id. art. 41. The seven-day limitation for temporary custody is new to the 1984 Regulation, presumably in response to abuses committed during the Cultural Revolution.

345. Beijing Domestic Service, Hubei PLA Group Disciplined for Finance Violations, Aug. 18, 1981, translated in F.B.I.S., Aug. 21, 1981, at P2.

346. Zhao, Beijing Military Region Moves Against Exam Fraud, Renmin Ribao, Mar. 22, 1984, at 4, translated in JPRS - CPS, June 28, 1984, at 110.

347. Military Criminal Law art. 2.

348. Criminal Procedure Law art. 3.

349. Arrest & Detention Act of the PRC, supra note 271, art. 8.

350. Criminal Procedure Law art. 92. Actual practice still falls short of these mandated time standards. See S. Leng & H. Chiu, supra note 261, at 89.

351. Criminal Procedure Law art. 32.

352. Id. art. 100.

353. Military Criminal Law art. 25.

354.   Zhang & Jim, [Studies in How To Determine Those Subject To Military Functional Offenses], 3 Faxue Yanjiu (Studies in Law) 28, 29-30 (1984).

355.   Id. at 31, 32. This position has been enacted in the U.S.S.R. Military Criminal Law, Dec. 25, 1958, art. 1, incorporated as art. 237 of the Criminal Code of the R.S.F.S.R., translated in H. Berman, Soviet Criminal Law and Procedure (1972). Joint crimes are treated in the PRC Criminal Law, art. 22.

356.   Criminal Procedure Law art. 110.

357.   Quoted in S..Leng & H. Chiu, supra note 261, at 95.

358.   Criminal Procedure Law art. 105; Tsien, supra note 2, at 182.

359.   Tsien, supra note 2, at 182.

360.   Id. Since 1983, assessors may be replaced with panel judges at the discretion of the trial court. S. Leng & H. Chiu, supra note 261, at 67.

361.   Criminal Procedure Law arts. 108-125.

362.   Id. art 111; Tsien, supra note 2, at 183.

363.   Criminal Procedure Law art. 120.

364.   Id. art. 121; Tsien, supra note 2, at 183.

365. According to official statistics for the first nine months of 1981, 99.7% of prosecutions brought by the people's procuracy at all levels were found guilty by the people's courts. S. Leng & H. Chiu, supra note 261, at 70.

366. Criminal Procedure Law arts. 129-143.

367. Id. art. 144,; Tsien, supra note 2, at 183.

368. Tsien, supra note 2, at 183.

369. Criminal Procedure Law arts. 59, 126-128.

370. Translated in Inside China Mainland, Nov. 1986, at 28.

371. Criminal Procedure Law, art. 60. Filing false accusations is a criminal offense under article 138 of the Criminal Law, and a disciplinary offense under article 21(15) of the PLA Discipline Regulation (1984).

372. Peking Domestic Service, supra note 269, at E22-23.

373. 2 People's China and International Law 1415 (J. Cohen & H. Chiu eds. 1974).

374. Protocol for the Prohibition of the Use in War of Asphyxiating, Poisonous or Other Gases, and of Bacteriological Methods of Warfare, June 17, 1925, 94 L.N.T.S. 71.

375. 1929 Geneva Conventions, 160 L.N.T.S. 383.

376. 2 People's China and International Law, supra note 373, at 1417.

377. Statement by the Central Committee of the Chinese Communist Party on Agreements and Negotiations Between the Kuomintang and Foreign Governments, Feb. 1, 1947, Hsin-hua jih-pao (New China Daily), Feb. 6, 1947, at 2, translated in U.S. Department of State, United States Relations With China 719, 720 (1949).

378. Common Program, supra note 168, art. 55.

379. On China's Recognition of the Protocol of June 17, 1925, Prohibiting Chemical and Biological Warfare; On China's Recognition of the 1949 Geneva Conventions, People's China, Aug. 1, 1952, at 33.

380. PRC Ratification of 1949 Geneva Conventions, Dec. 28, 1956, 260 U.N.T.S. 442.

381. PRC Ratification of 1981 UN Conventional Weapons Convention, 1982 [Chinese Yearbook of International Law] (Chinese International Law Society) 491.

382. Official Records of the Diplomatic Conference on the Reaffirmation and Development of International Humanitarian Law Applicable in Armed Conflicts 83 (Bern 1978).

383. PRC Accession to Protocols, 237 Int'l Rev. Red Cross 315 (1983).

384. Sun Tzu, supra note 28, at 76. Sun Tzu's disciple, Chang Yu, explained the practical basis for this humanitarian rule: "All the soldiers taken must be cared for with magnanimity and sincerity so that they may be used by us." Id.

385. Cited in 2 People's China and International Law, supra note 373, at 1414.

386. Resolution, supra note 92, at 185.

387. Id.

388. See supra text accompanying notes 88 & 91, and note 92.

389. U.K. Ministry of Defence, Treatment of British Prisoners of War in Korea (1955), reprinted in H. Levie, Documents on Prisoners of War doc. 134, at 651, 652 (60 Naval War College International Law Studies 1979).

390. See generally id. and U.S. Department of Defense, P.O.W.: The Fight Continues After the Battle (1955), reprinted in H. Levie, supra note 389, doc. 131, at 643.

391. Senate Comm. on Government Operations, Korean War Atrocities, S. Rep. No. 848, 83d Cong., 2d Sess. 13-15 (1954). Of 7,140 U.S. P.O.W.s in the Korean War, 2,701 died in captivity (about 38%) D. Rees, Korea: The Limited War 461 (1964). In contrast, only 4% of U.S. and U.K. P.O.W.s held during the Second World War by Nazi Germany and Fascist Italy died in captivity (9,348 of 235,473). International Military Tribunal for the Far East, The Tokyo War Crimes Trial, Nov. 1948, reprinted in 2 The Law of War 1029, 1056 (L. Friedman ed. 1972). Detailed records of war crimes committed by the Chinese and North Korean Communists were collected by the War Crimes Division of the U.S. Army Judge Advocate Section in Korea. By the end of the conflict, reports of war crimes committed

by the Chinese (not including those attributed to the North Koreans) totalled 4,922, of which 3,279 were committed against U.S. personnel. 3,139 of the total reports (2,178 U.S.) were classified as "probable war crimes." As of 30 June 1953, 439 case files had been prepared with a view toward prosecution. U.S. Army Judge Advocate Section, Korean Communications Zone, War Crimes Division, Interim Historical Report 43, 49 (June 30, 1953, copies on file in U.S. Army Judge Advocate General's School Library).

392. Ch'en T'i-ch'iang, Unconditional Repatriation – An Inviolable Principle of the Geneva Convention, People's China, Jan. 16, 1953, at 26-28.

393. Of 20,344 Chinese P.O.W.s, 5,777 returned to the PRC, and 14,567 went to Taiwan. J. Goulden, Korea: The Untold Story of the War 647 (1982). Many of the defectors may have been former Nationalist troops impressed into the PLA. Others may have been motivated by fear of punishment under the long-standing Communist prohibition on surrendering, now codified as art. 19 of the Military Criminal Law (punishable by 3 years to life imprisonment).

394. 2 People's China and International Law, supra note 373, at 1573-75.

395. 210 Int'l Rev. Red Cross 162 (1979).

396. 211 Int'l Rev. Red Cross 211 (1979).

397. Chen, China's War Against Vietnam, 1979: A Military Analysis, J. E. Asian Affairs, Sp./Sum. 1983, at 233, 257.

398. Geneva Convention for the Amelioration of the Conditions of the Wounded and Sick in Armed Forces in the Field, Aug. 12, 1949 [hereinafter GWS], art. 49, 75 U.N.T.S. 31; Geneva Convention for the Amelioration of the Condition of Wounded, Sick and Shipwrecked Members of Armed Forces at Sea, Aug. 12, 1949 [hereinafter GWS Sea], art. 50, 75 U.N.T.S. 85; Geneva Convention Relative to the Treatment of Prisoners of War, Aug. 12, 1949 [hereinafter GPW], art. 129, 75 U.N.T.S. 135; Geneva Convention Relative to the Protection of Civilian Persons in Time of War, Aug. 12, 1949 [hereinafter GC], art. 146, 75 U.N.T.S. 287.

399. GWS art. 50; GWS Sea art. 51; GPW art. 130; GC art. 147.

400. See, supra text accompanying notes 87 & 388.

401. GWS art. 49; GWS Sea art. 50; GPW art. 129; GC art. 146.

402. GPW art. 129.

403. P. Piccigallo, The Japanese on Trial 173 (1979).

404. Law Governing the Trial of War Criminals, Oct. 24, 1946, in 14 Law Reports of Trials of War Criminals 152 (1949).

405. P. Piccigallo, supra note 403, at 170.

406. NPC Decision on Japanese Criminals, June 21, 1956, reprinted in 2 People's China and International Law, supra note 373, at 1590.

407. Id.

408. New China News Agency, Japanese War Criminals Tried in Shenyang, June 21, 1956, reprinted in 2 People's China and International Law, supra note 373, at 1591-93.

409. New China News Agency, 355 Japanese Criminals Set Free, June 22, 1956, reprinted in 2 People's China and International Law, supra note 373, at 1594.

410. Particularly those providing: "No moral or physical coercion may be exerted on a prisoner of war in order to induce him to admit himself guilty of the act of which he is accused." GPW art. 99.

411. Resolution, supra note 92, at 182.

412. See supra note 93.

413. See, supra note 159 and accompanying text.

414. PLA Discipline Regulation (1984) art. 2(1).

415. See supra text accompanying notes 345 & 346.

416. See Li & Wang, Adhere to the Principle That All Men Are Equal Before the Law, Safeguard the Authority and Dignity of the Law, Red Flag, June 16, 1986, at 24-27, translated in Joint Publications Research Service, China Report: Red Flag, Aug. 7, 1986, at 42, 43, 45-46. Equality before the law is now proclaimed in the Constitution (1982), art. 23: "All citizens of the PRC are equal before the Law"; and in the Organic Law of the People's Courts, art. 5: "In conducting trial, the people's courts treat all citizens equally according to the law, irrespective of nationality, race, sex,

occupation, social background, religious belief, education, financial status or length of residence, and without allowing any special privileges."

417. PLA Discipline Regulation (1975) art. 3(c).

418. Id. art. 16.

419. Beijing Domestic Service, Yu Qiuli Proposes 'Eight Prohibitions' for PLA, Aug. 8, 1986, translated in F.B.I.S., Aug. 11, 1986, at K1.

420. Li & Wang, supra note 416, at 46.

APPENDIX A

PROVISIONAL REGULATIONS OF THE PEOPLE'S REPUBLIC OF CHINA ON PUNISHING SERVICEMEN WHO COMMIT OFFENSES AGAINST THEIR DUTIES.* [Adopted 10 June 1981 by the Standing Committee of the 5th National People's Congress at its 19th session]

Article 1

On the basis of the guiding ideology and fundamental principles of the "Criminal Law of the People's Republic of China," these regulations are formulated with a view to punishing servicemen for offenses they commit against their duties, educating them to conscientiously carry out their duties and strenghtening the combat capability of army units.

Article 2

Any act of an active duty PLA serviceman that infringes on his duties and endangers the state's military interests and is punishable by law is considered a serviceman's offense against his duties. However, in cases of markedly mild offenses and when not too much harm has been caused, the act is not considered an offense and will be dealt with in accordance with military discipline.

Article 3

Any person who violates the regulations on using firearms and equipment and causes serious accidents arising from his negligence and resulting in severe injury or death of others may in serious cases be

---

*Chinese text in 12 State Council Bulletin (1981). Translation in Foreign Broadcast Information Service, Daily Report: China, June 12, 1981, at K 1.

sentenced to fixed-term imprisonment of not more than 3 years of detention at hard labor, and in cases with particularly serious consequences to fixed-term imprisonment of not less than 3 years and not more than 7 years.

Article 4

Any person who violates the law and regulations on guarding the state's military secrets by betraying or losing important state military secrets may in serious cases be sentenced to fixed-term imprisonment of not more than 7 years or detention at hard labor.

Any person who commits the above offense during wartime may be sentenced to fixed-term imprisonment of not less than 3 years and not more than 10 years, and in particularly serious cases to fixed-term imprisonment of not less than 10 years or life imprisonment.

Any person who steals, collects or furnishes military secrets for enemies or foreigners may be sentenced to fixed-term imprisonment of not less than 10 years, life imprisonment or death.

Article 5

Any personnel in command or on duty who causes serious consequences by leaving his post or neglecting his duties may be sentenced to fixed-term imprisonment of not more than 7 years or detention at hard labor.

Any person who commits the above offense during wartime may be sentenced to fixed-term imprisonment of not less than 5 years.

Article 6

Any person who deserts the army in violation of the military service law may in serious cases be sentenced to fixed-term imprisonment of not more than 3 years or detention at hard labor.

Any person who commits the above offense during wartime may be sentenced to fixed-term imprisonment of not less than 3 years and not more than 7 years.

Article 7

Any person who crosses the boundary (border) illegally to flee the country may be sentenced to fixed-term imprisonment of not more than 3 years or detention at hard labor, and in serious cases to fixed-term imprisonment of not less than 3 years and not more than 10 years.

During wartime, offenders may be subject to heavier punishment.

Article 8

Any serviceman on active duty at the border or coastal defense line who practices favoritism or commits other irregularities or allows another person to cross the boundary (border) without authorization may be sentenced to fixed-term imprisonment of not more than 5 years or detention at hard labor, and in serious cases to imprisonment of not less than 5 years. During wartime, the punishment may be more severe.

Article 9

Any serviceman who abuses his power of office to maltreat or persecute a subordinate and whose offenses are so vile as to have caused serious injuries or other serious consequences may be sentenced to fixed-term imprisonment of not more than 5 years or detention at hard labor. For offenses that result in the death of a person, offenders may be sentenced to fixed-term imprisonment of not less than 5 years.

Article 10

Any person who resorts to violence or threat to obstruct command personnel or personnel on shift or station duty from performing their duties may be sentenced to fixed-term imprisonment of not more than 5 years or detention at hard labor, and in serious cases to fixed-term imprisonment of not less than 5 years. In especially serious cases or in cases of serious injuries or deaths resulting from such offenses, offenders may be sentenced to life imprisonment or death. During wartime, the punishment may be more severe.

Article 11

In cases of theft of weapons, equipment or military supplies, offenders may be sentenced to fixed-term imprisonment of not more than 5 years or detention at hard labor, and in serious cases, to fixed-term imprisonment of not less than 5 years and not more than 10 years. In especially serious cases, offenders may be sentenced to fixed-term imprisonment of not less than 10 years or life imprisonment. During wartime, the punishment may be more severe, and offenders may be given the death sentence if the offenses are especially serious.

Article 12

Any person who commits the crime of sabotaging weapons, equipment or military installations may be sentenced to fixed-term imprisonment of not more than 3 years or detention at hard labor. In cases of sabotage of major weapons, equipment or military installations, offenders may be sentenced to fixed-term imprisonment of not less than 3 years and not more than 10 years. In especially serious cases, offenders may be sentenced to fixed-term imprisonment of not less than 10 years, life imprisonment or death. During wartime the punishment may be more severe.

Article 13

Any serviceman who deliberately inflicts injuries to himself in order to evade his military obligations during wartime may be sentenced to fixed-term imprisonment of not more than 3 years, and in serious cases to fixed-term imprisonment of not less than 3 years and not more than 7 years.

Article 14

Any person who fabricates rumors to mislead others and undermine army morale during wartime may be sentenced to fixed-term imprisonment of not more than 3 years, and in serious cases to fixed-term imprisonment of not less than 3 years but not more than 10 years.

Any person who colludes with the enemy to spread rumors so as to mislead others and undermine army morale may be sentenced to fixed-term imprisonment of not less than 10 years or life imprisonment. In especially serious cases, offenders may be given the death sentence.

Article 15

Any person who is directly responsible for deliberate abandonment of wounded on the battlefield, particularly in those cases that are considered abominable, may be sentenced to fixed-term imprisonment of not more than 3 years.

Article 16

All servicemen who are afraid of fighting and desert from the battlefield will be sentenced to 3 years' imprisonment or less; in serious cases, they will be sentenced to 3 to 10 years' imprisonment; and in cases which caused major losses in battle or war, they will be sentenced to 10 years to life imprisonment or death.

Article 17

All servicemen who disobey orders during a battle, thus jeopardizing the outcome of a war, will be sentenced to 3 to 10 years' imprisonment, and in cases of serious harm to the battle or war effort they will be sentenced to 10 years to life imprisonment or death.

Article 18

All servicemen who intentionally make a false report about the military situation and fake military orders, thus jeopardizing military operations, will be sentenced to 3 to 10 years' imprisonment, and in cases of serious harm to the battle and war effort they will be sentenced to 10 years to life imprisonment or death.

Article 19

All servicemen who are afraid of death in battle and voluntarily lay down weapons and surrender to the enemy will be sentenced to 3 to 10 years' imprisonment, and in cases of a serious nature they will be sentenced to 10 years to life imprisonment.

All servicemen who, after surrendering to the enemy, help the enemy will be sentenced to 10 years to life imprisonment or death.

Article 20

All servicemen who plunder and harm innocent residents in military operational areas will be sentenced to 7 years or less; in serious cases, they will be sentenced to more than 7 years' imprisonment; and in cases of a particularly serious nature, they will be sentenced to life imprisonment or death.

Article 21

All servicemen who seriously maltreat captives will be sentenced to 3 years' imprisonment or less.

Article 22

In times of war, servicemen who are sentenced to 3 years' imprisonment or less with a reprieve because there is no actual danger may be allowed to atone for their crimes by performing good services. When they have performed really good services, the original sentence may be rescinded, and they will no longer be considered criminals.

Article 23

All servicemen on active duty who commit crimes not listed in these regulations will be handled in accordance with the related articles of "The Criminal Law of the People's Republic of China."

Article 24

As to servicemen who commit serious crimes, their decorations, medals and titles of honor may be recalled, in addition to their being punished.

Article 25

All staff members and workers of the military establishment who commit crimes listed in these regulations will be punished in accordance with these regulations.

Article 26

These regulations will become effective as of 1 January 1982.

APPENDIX B

CHINESE PEOPLE'S LIBERATION ARMY DISCIPLINE REGULATION*

[Promulgated 27 January 1984 by the
Central Military Commission of the People's
Republic of China]

Chapter I General Principles

Article 1.   The discipline of the Chinese People's Liberation Army is a strict discipline based on political consciousness. It is an important factor for the combat effectiveness of the Army and a guarantee for uniting ourselves, winning victories over the enemy, and accomplishing all tasks. Members of the whole Army must consciously and strictly observe military discipline, faithfully and loyally fulfill their sacred duty of defending the socialist motherland and the people under all kinds of arduous and dangerous conditions, firmly implement orders, and must not violate any discipline.

Article 2.   Basic content of the Chinese People's Liberation Army discipline:

    1.   Implementing the line, principles, and policies of the Communist Party of China, and observing the state's Constitution, laws and regulations;

---

* Chinese text in 1985 Yearbook on Chinese Communism 9-15 to 9-22 (Taipei: Institute for the Study of Chinese Communist Problems). Translated by Daniel Chen.

2.   Implementing the various orders, rules, and regulations of the Army;

3.   Implementing orders, directives and instructions of the higher level;

4.   Implementing the Three Main Rules of Discipline and the Eight Points for Attention.

The Three Main Rules of Discipline: (1) Obey orders in all your actions; (2) Do not take a single needle or piece of threat from the masses; (3) Turn in everything captured.

The Eight Points for Attention: (1) Speak politely; (2) Pay fairly for what you buy; (3) Return everything you borrow; (4) Pay for anything you damage; (5) Do not hit or swear at people; (6) Do not damage crops; (7) Do not take liberties with women; (8) Do not ill-treat captives.

Article 3.   To maintain and consolidate the discipline of our army, all members of the Army must be educated in its morale, laws, regulations, and discipline.

The execution of discipline must be clear-cut concerning rewards and punishments.   To those who distinguish themselves in accomplishing the mission, obeying and upholding discipline, appropriate rewards should be granted.   To those who violate discipline, appropriate punishment should be given, depending on the situation.

Article 4.   The leadership at every level has the direct responsibility to maintain discipline, and has the authority to grant either rewards or punishments in accordance with these regulations. All leaders at all levels must serve as models in strictly obeying, maintaining and protecting discipline. When administering rewards or punishments, leaders must apply the principles and facts in a timely and appropriate manner, without partiality, not substituting sentiments for policy. In general situations, all punishments and rewards should be submitted to the Party committee (branch) for discussion and determination, and be carried out by the leadership.

Article 5.   Military personnel must conscientiously obey and maintain discipline. When one violates discipline and is stopped and dissuaded by others, he should make immediate corrections; the exemplary behavior or deeds of others observed should be dilligently learned from and applied; upon observing other military personnel violating discipline, one should dissuade and stop them; upon observing others violating the law, one must step forward and persistently stop it. All the above-mentioned circumstances should be timely reported to superiors.

Chapter II <u>Rewards</u> (omitted)

Chapter III <u>Punishments</u>

Section 1. Purpose of punishments, categories
and requirements.

Article 20.   Punishment is an auxilliary educational means to maintain
and consolidate discipline. Its purpose is to learn from
past mistakes to avoid future ones and to cure the illness
to save the patient, to strengthen unity and to heighten
combat effectiveness.

Article 21.   Categories of punishment.

1.   Warning;

2.   Serious warning;

3.   Demerit;

4.   Major demerit;

5.   Demotion from position (rank);

6.   Dismissal from office;

7.   Dismissal from military status.

Demotion from position (rank), generally demote one
position or one rank; cadres demoted from position should
at the same time be demoted in salary. For enlisted men,

B-4

the punishment of demotion from position applies to sergeants, demotion of rank applies to volunteers, dismissal from office applies to sergeants and deputy sergeants.

Article 22. To those who perpetrate one of the discipline-violating acts listed below, which result in damages or adverse effects, or violate laws, or commit criminal violations of the law but, according to the law, they are exempted from being charged for criminal responsibility, should, according to the circumstances, be given education and criticism or appropriate disciplinary punishment.

1. Violating the policy of the Party and the Constitution, laws and regulations of the state;

2. Violating and disobeying orders, violating codes, regulations, institutions and systems;

3. Displaying a negative attitude in combat, cowardice in combat, failure to grasp combat opportunities;

4. Acting individually without orders or coordination from superiors and thereby hindering coordinated operations;

5. Damaging or losing public property, weapons, or equipment, or causing incidents due to violations of institutions;

6. Revelation of state and military secrets;

7.   Failure to perform duties, delaying work;

8.   Absence without leave, or failure to return from leave on time;

9.   Threatening superiors or others with weapons;

10. Fighting, or disturbing the public order;

11. Obscene or indecent conduct, dissolute behavior;

12. Theft of public or private property;

13. Gambling, smuggling, speculation;

14. Seeing a danger and not assisting;

15. Counterblows and vengeance, framing others, making false accusations, or creating rumors;

16. Unprincipled behavior, condoning wrongdoers and violations;

17. Suppressing democracy and physically punishing subordinates;

18. Making falsities and fakes, and deceiving superiors;

19. Violating discipline in other aspects.

Those who have violated the state's law so as to necessitate indictment for criminal responsibiltiy shall be transferred to the judicial departments for trial according to the law.

Section 2. Authority for punishment.

Article 23.   Authority for punishment of enlisted men (including voluntary soldiers):

The company commander and political instructor have authority to issue warning.

The battalion commander and political instructor have authority to issue warning and serious warning.

The regiment commander and political commissar have authority to issue warning, serious warning, demerit, major demerit, demotion from position, demotion from rank, or dismissal from position.

The division commander and political commissar, the army commander and political commissar, and the military region commander and political commissar have authority over all categories of punishment.

Article 24.   Authority for punishment of cadres of platoon-level or higher:

The battalion commander and political instructor have authority to issue warning to platoon-level cadres.

The regiment commander and political commissar have authority to issue warning, serious warning, demerit and major demerit to platoon-level cadres; for company-level cadres they have authority to issue warning and serious warning.

The division commander and political commissar have authority to issue warning, serious warning, demerit and major demerit to cadres of battalion-level or below.

The army commander and political commissar have authority to issue warning, serious warning, demerit, and major demerit to cadres of regiment-level or below.

The military region commander and political commissar have authority over all categories of punishment for cadres of battalion-level or below, and have authority to issue warning, serious warning, demerit and major demerit to cadres of division and regiment level.

Enforcement of demotion from position, demotion of rank, or dismissal from position shall be carried out by authorities responsible for appointment and dismissal.

Authority for punishment of dismissal from military status for cadres of regiment-level and above, and authority for punishment of cadres of army level and above, is vested in the Chairman of the State Central Military Commission.

Demotion of rank shall be enforced in accordance with the Chinese People's Liberation Army Regulations on the Service of Officers.

Article 25.   (omitted)

Article 26.   (omitted)

Article 27.   All general headquarters, branches of the armed forces, armed service branches, and equivalent units have the same authority of punitive action as that vested in the military region.

Article 28.   Deputy commanders at every level have the authority of punitive action when they are acting as the commander.

Section 3. Enforcement of Punishment.

Article 29.   Punitive actions must be determined with solemnity and care. Especially during wartime, it is essential to maintain the aggressive attitude of combat leaders. All punishments imposed by superiors on their subordinates must be based on investigation, research, and clear resolution of any mistaken facts, as well as the following:

1.   A comprehensive and historical evaluation must be made of the facts, nature, details, circumstances, and influences of the errors committed, as well as the violator's past performance and his degree of recognition of the mistake. It is necessary to listen to both the opinions of the masses and the statement of the violator. The violator should be educated to repent to the wrongdoing.

2.   Each wrongdoer should receive only one punishment.

Article 30.   Superiors are to handle violations in a timely manner. In general, punitive actions should be administered within two months. If the case is especially complicated, or other unusual circumstances necessitate extension of this time limit, the case should be submitted to the higher level for approval.

Article 31.   In determining punishment it is necessary to first meet with the violator and hear his statement. If the violator does not accept his punishment, he may petition for appeal within ten days. Execution of punishment will not be suspended during the petition period.

Article 32.   Announcement of the decision and of the punishment, in order to educate the violator and the troops, may be made as follows: face-to-face, before the troops, in meetings, or in writing.

Persevere in giving violators persuasive education and assistance, do not discriminate against them, and prohibit physical punishment, scolding, or indirect means of physical punishment. Insulting personal dignity is especially prohibited.

Article 33.   Superiors of every level must constantly supervise punishments administered by subordinates. Whenever they discover any inappropriate punishments, superiors should direct subordinates to correct them promptly. All punishments administered shall be recorded and filed.

Chapter IV. Accusation and Appeal

Article 34.   Accusation and appeal are the democratic rights of servicemen, which are designed to bring into play the role of supervision of the masses, and to guarantee that punishments will be enforced correctly.

Article 35.   Soldiers have the right to make accusations against those who have perpetrated offenses against law and discipline. Those who consider the punitive actions taken against them to be improper have the right to appeal. Accusations and appeals should be based on facts and should not falsely accuse others.

Accusations and appeals may be submitted through channels, or bypassing channels. Those bypassing channels should be submitted in writing.

Soldiers' accusations against nonmilitary personnel should be reported to political organs, which will assess the situation and, if necessary, render assistance.

Article 36.   The accused have the right to defense, but they should not try to make things difficult for, or try to hinder, the accuser in submitting accusations, nor should they attempt counterattacks or revenge.

Article 37.   The rights of accusation and appeal of military personnel should be fully protected. Superiors of every level and any organ shall not detain or stop accusations and appeals made by military personnel, nor will they cover for or protect the accused.   If the accusation should be transferred to other relevant departments, it should be transferred to a superior of the accused. If an appeal is proved true, and the original punishment was inappropriate, it should be corrected.

Article 38.   Superiors of every level must immediately investigate and handle accusations and appeals made by military personnel. The period of handling generally should not exceed two months. The person making an accusation or appeal should be informed of the disposition in a timely manner.

Chapter V. Handling of Special Cases

Article 39.   (omitted)

Article 40.   (omitted)

Article 41.   Soldiers who have manifested evident signs that they might desert out of fear of punishment, or that they might commit violence or ʹsuicide, etc., may be placed in temporary custody.

Temporary custody is a preventive measure, ordinarily involving isolation or appointment of personnel to watch over the actions of the detainee. Those under temporary custody should receive education. No torture is allowed. The detainee's problem should be investigated and handled appropriately. Dispositions should be reported to superiors in a timely manner. The period of temporary custody generally should not exceed seven days. If extension is necessary it should be approved by superiors, but the accumulation should not exceed 15 days.

Authority for imposing temporary custody is as follows:

Soldiers—approved by regiment commander.

Platoon and company cadres—approved by division commander.

Battalion and regiment cadres—approved by army commander.

Division cadres—approved by military region commander.

Army level cadres and above—approved by State Central Military Commission.

Article 42.   Under emergencies commanders of every level are authorized to temporarily remove from their positions incompetent subordinate cadres, and to appoint substitutes, but they should report to their superiors as soon as possible and be held responsible for their actions.

Article 43.   Upon discovering criminal acts such as deserting in combat, mutiny, violent acts and murder, and when there is no time to report the incident, soldiers should take immediate measures to stop it, report it to their superiors afterwards, and be held responsible for their actions.

Chapter VI. Supplementary Articles

Article 44.   (omitted)

Article 45.   (omitted)

Article 46.   (omitted)

Article 47.   (omitted)

Article 48.   These regulations apply to active duty military personnel, to military staff members and to military establishment workers.

APPENDIX C

PROVISIONAL ORGANIZATIONAL REGULATIONS OF THE MILITARY COURTS OF THE CHINESE SOVIET REPUBLIC*

CENTRAL EXECUTIVE COMMITTEE OF THE CHINESE SOVIET REPUBLIC   ORDER number 3

In order to protect the rights of fighters, commanders, and personnel within the Red Army, and to uphold the Red Army's iron discipline, the Executive Committee specially promulgates "The Provisional Organizational Regulations of the Military Courts of the Soviet Republic's Red Army." The regulations promulgated here shall take effect as of 15 Feburary 1932. After the Revolutionary Military Central Committee receives this order, it shall be transmitted to the headquarters of units of the Red Army and militia, and these shall organize military courts in accordance with the specifications of these regulations in order to administer all criminal adjudications within the Red Army and to render judgments regarding them.

Chairman	Mao Tse-tung
Vice-Chairmen	Hsiang Ying
	Chang Kuo-t'ao

1 February 1932

---

* Original in Shih-sou tzu-liao-shih kung-fei tzu-liao (Hoover Institution, microfilm, 1960) no. 008.5525/3754/0553, reel 7, item 15. Translated by Gary White (revised).

PROVISIONAL ORGANIZATIONAL REGULATIONS OF THE MILITARY COURTS OF THE CHINESE SOVIET REPUBLIC

Chapter I: General Principles

Article 1: All members of the Red Army, guerilla bands, independent divisions and regiments, companies of Communist (Red) guards, and assorted armed groups in military service, no matter if they are military personel or function in some other capacity, shall have their cases adjudicated by the military courts if they violate the criminal law, the military criminal law, or some other law. However, this does not apply to those whose actions are violations of common discipline but not of the law.

Article 2: In battle zones, the illegal actions of residents will be judged by the military courts whether the infraction was against the military criminal (code) or some other law; activities such as spying or espionage, if within a battle zone, shall also be judged by the military courts.

Article 3: Each level of military courts must be organized according to the provisions of these regulations.

Chapter II: The System of Organization of the Military Courts

Article 4: Military courts shall be divided into the following four types: (i) primary military courts, (ii) primary field military courts, (iii) superior military courts, and (iv) the Supreme Military Judicial Conference.

Article 5: The primary military courts shall be established within the headquarters of the Red Army, division headquarters, the headquarters of military districts, and the headquarters of independent divisions; primary field military courts shall be established within the headquarters of the highest leadership in the battle-zone.

Article 6: The superior military courts shall be established within the Central Revoluntionary Military Committee.

Article 7: The Supreme Military Judicial Conference shall be established within the Supreme Court.

Article 8: The primary military courts and the primary field military courts shall be subordinate to the superior military courts; and the superior military courts shall be subordinate to the Supreme Court.

(Note 1) Until the Supreme Court is established, the Provisional Central Government shall temporarily organize a court to resolve cases to be reviewed by the Supreme Military Judicial Conference.

(Note 2) For Soviet territory that is not yet contiguous with the central Soviet territory, the superior military courts established in the highest military committees shall also have the authority of courts of last resort.

Chapter III: The Composition of the Military Courts

Article 9: Primary military courts shall be composed of a (chief) judge and two (panel) judges, who shall comprise a judicial committee. The Superior military courts shall consist of a judicial committee composed of a (chief) judge, an assistant judge, and three panel judges, and (such committee) shall see to the necessary arrangements of the primary military courts. The Supreme Court shall determine what people shall comprise the Supreme Judicial Military Conference; the participation of representatives of the Central Revolutionary Military Committee is essential.

Article 10: The judge and the panel judges of the primary military courts shall be elected from representatives of the officers and soldiers and shall be approved by the superior military courts. The judge and the panel judges of the superior military court shall be nominated by the Central Revolutionary Military Committee and shall pass the approval of the Supreme Court.

Article 11: The commander of any level military unit may not concurrently serve as a judge or a panel judge of a military court.

Article 12: The court for the adjudications at the primary military court shall consist of three people. The judge shall be chairperson and the other two shall be assessors. Whenever cases are being examined by the superior military courts as a court of first instance, assessors must be used. However, for final reviews, no assessors shall be used; rather, the court shall consist of the presiding judge and the panel judges.

Article 13: Assessors shall be selected from among the officers and soldiers, and be changed once a week. For the period they act as assessors, they may be relieved of their military duties; when the assessor period is over, they shall return to the work of their original unit.

Article 14: Each level of military court must employ clerks and other (suitably) skilled personnel.

(Note 1) If the caseload is light, the number of members of the military courts can be decreased; the primary military courts may be provided with as few as one judge. The superior military courts may be provided with as few as one judge and one panel judge.

(Note 2) If the case to be judged is simple and does not involve anything essential, a single panel judge may decide it.

Chapter IV: The Jurisdiction of Military Courts and their Judicial Procedures

Article 15: The primary military courts shall judge as a court of first instance all of the cases of crimes of military leadership below the rank of division commander, fighters, and all staff serving within the military units.

Article 16: The primary military courts for the militia shall judge the military cases of the militia for the whole province.

Article 17: Primary field military courts shall judge all cases in areas where war is on, but shall still be courts of first hearing.

Article 18: The superior military courts are courts of last resort for judging cases already decided by primary military courts but appealed; at the same time they are courts of first hearing for the cases of command staff above the rank of division commander.

Article 19: The Supreme Military Judicial Conference is the court of last resort for judging cases already decided by superior military courts but appealed; at the same time they are the court that shall judge personnel doing important military work who are above the rank of corps commander.

Article 20: Except for the Supreme Military Judicial Conference, for the decided cases of all the other levels of military courts, all the accused shall have the right to appeal within the appeal period prescribed in the verdict. The time limit for appeals shall be from 72 hours to one month, the appeal period is to be determined by the court deciding the particular case at the time.

Article 21: In all cases with verdicts calling for the death penalty, even if the accused does not initiate an appeal, the court judging the particular case must submit the court records to the higher court for confirmation (of the verdict).

(Note) Under extraordinary military conditions a judgment may be executed, and copies of the file of the case sent to a higher court for subsequent confirmation.

Article 22: The judging of cases must be done in a format open to the public, allowing officers, soldiers, and military staff to observe; however, if a case involves military secrets, a secret form of hearing may be selected, but the announcement of the decision must be public.

Article 23: When hearing a case, the court does not necessarily have to hear the case at its normal location. (The court) can go to the location of the military unit and the place of work of the transgressor to decide the case.

Chapter V: The Military Procuracy - Its Organization and Responsibilities

Article 24: Wherever there are primary and superior military courts, there shall be established, respectively, a primary military procuracy and a superior military procuracy.

Article 25: The primary military procuracy shall have one procurator, one assistant procurator and several investigators. The superior military procuracy shall have one procurator general, two assistant procurators, and several investigators. In addition, five staff for assorted skilled positions such as secretaries and clerks may be employed.

(Note) The staff personnel of the military procuracy can, depending upon the military units situations, be decreased from time to time.

Article 26: If the commanders of any level or political commissars discover evidence of an illegal act in a military unit, they may execute an arrest of the transgressor and deliver him over to the appropriate level military procuracy for investigation.

Article 27: The military procuracy shall be the institution responsible for investigations and inquests into military crimes. All cases, except for simple cases that are clear-cut and do not need further investigation, shall be sent to the military procuracy of the appropriate level for investigation. After the military procuracy has finished its investigation and issued its conclusion, they shall send the case to the military court for a hearing.

Article 28. The military procuracy is the prosecuting institution representing the state in cases of military crimes. It may investigate all cases of illegal activity within or relating to the military. Moreover, it may initiate a public complaint in a court, and during trial it may represent the state in appearing in court and lodging charges.

Article 29: During the investigation of a case, the procurator shall have sole authority to interrogate anyone connected with the case.

Article 30: At the time of summons for interrogation a court writ, an arrest warrant, or a procuracy writ may be used.

(Note 1) A military court may use only court writs and arrest warrants.

(Note 2) Headquarters of corps, divisions, and other military organizations in places of the competence of military courts should allocate personnel for use in the procuracy.

Chapter VI: Funding

Article 31: The costs of the military courts and military procuracies shall be provided for by the appropriate military unit according to a budget.

Chapter VII: Supplement

Article 32: These regulations are the public order of the Central Executive Committee.

Article 33: The Central Executive Committee shall have the power to revise these regulations from time to time or to suspend them.

Article 34: From the day that these regulations are publicly promulgated, they shall be in force.

Central Executive Committee

Chairman   Mao Tse-tung

Vice-Chairmen   Hsiang Ying

                  Chang Kuo-t'ao